tabby weave

slitweave

selvedge
tied ground weft

selvedge
parallel wrapping

weft-faced plainweave

curved wefts

warp loop fringe

dovetailing

countered weft twining

net fringe

interlocking

wrapping with coloured weft

plaited fringe

Dhurries

Nada Chaldecott

Photographs by Jamie Govier

Dhurries

History • Pattern • Technique • Identification

With 265 illustrations, 248 in colour

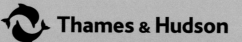
Thames & Hudson

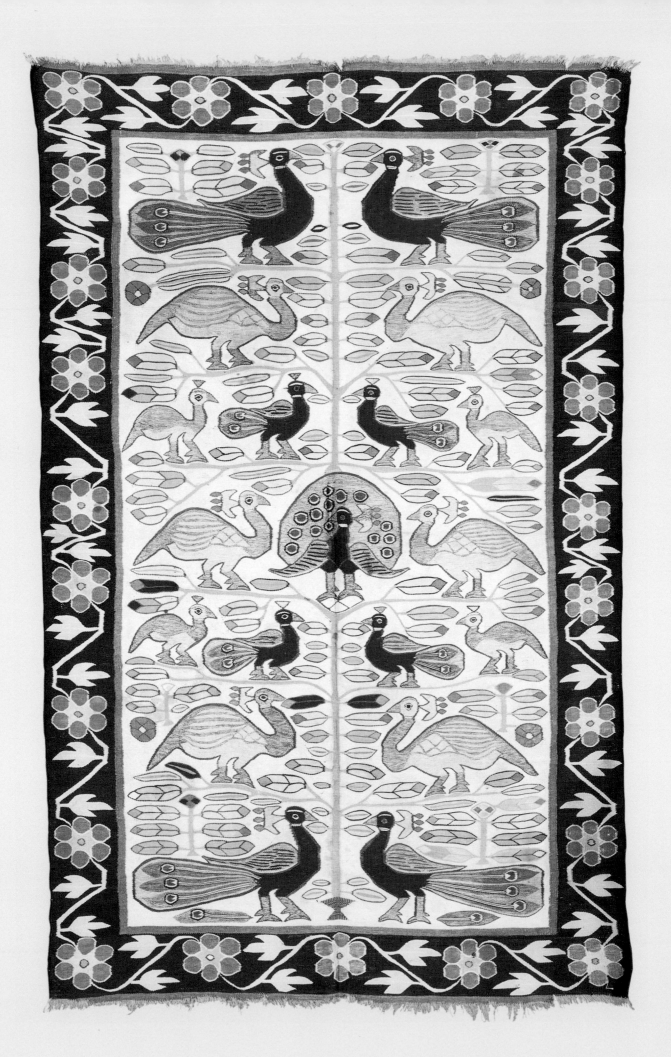

Contents

1

Half-title (p. 1) Detail of triple central medallion dhurrie, Multan, West Punjab (Pakistan), late 19th century.

2

Frontispiece (p. 2) Terrace, Bagru House, Jaipur, covered with small blue and white striped dhurries. T. C. Goel/Samurai Collection. A *chaupar* dhurrie is on the bed. Private collection.

3

Opposite Peacock dhurrie, northern Deccan, *c.* 1910. (also reproduced on p. 67). T. C. Goel/Samurai Collection.

First published in the United Kingdom in 2003 by Thames & Hudson Ltd
181A High Holborn, London WC1V 7QX

www.thamesandhudson.com

British Library Cataloguing-in-Publication Data
A catalogue record for this book is available from the British Library

ISBN 0-500-51138-1

Printed and bound in Hong Kong by C & C Offset

Introduction

The strong appeal of the dhurrie arises from its wonderful use of colour and its simplicity of design. Art historians have, however, been more impressed with the knotted carpets, made of prestigious silk or wool, and regard the flatweave cotton dhurrie as the carpet's poor relation. In India the dhurrie is popularly seen merely as a striped cotton floor-covering for everyday use. Yet it is very rewarding to study this strikingly colourful and often abstract art form, which relates so closely to our contemporary notion of art. In this book I hope to show not only the important function of the dhurrie in everyday life, but also the long established design traditions, and the rich variety of designs of this quintessential Indian art form. The dhurrie reached its apogee in the nineteenth and early twentieth centuries, and, for this reason, I have taken all my examples from the period between 1860 and the 1940s.

One cannot approach the study of the dhurrie without a knowledge of Indian floor designs, the woven reed mat designs, the use of animal skins, and the way in which the dhurrie is related to all these as well as to the knotted carpet.

Floor Paintings

Floor decoration in India has its origin in ritual. For Indian women the home is the most sacred space. Harmony and prosperity are the key factors for the well-being of the family, and the house must therefore be protected from evil spirits. For this purpose the tradition of decorating walls and floors with designs is widespread in Hindu and tribal communities. Their object is to invoke the appropriate deities from the Hindu pantheon.[1] In this simple art form, strong beliefs and a love of ornamentation create an intricate decorative vocabulary found in even the humblest

4

Tamil woman decorating the threshold of a house for a religious festival, Bangalore.

5

Holi, the spring festival, Pahari, 3rd quarter
of the 18th century. Indian Museum, Calcutta.

dwelling. In the great Hindu epic the *Ramayana*, the goddess Sita
paints her home with sacred designs.[2] For everyday rituals the
women decorate the mud floor with a ground rice paste – white is
a pure and sacred colour (4 & 6). Different designs and symbols
are used each day,[3] and the threshold is the most significant area.

Coloured pigments are used for the more important religious
festivals, such as Holi, the spring festival of colour (5), and
Diwali, the autumn festival of light. Unfortunately, natural dyes
are now often replaced by synthetic dyes. Floor decorations, vari-
ously called *rangoli* in Hindi, *mandanas* in Rajasthan and *kolam* in the
Tamil language of south India, also celebrate special occasions,
such as crop-planting, harvest, monsoon, the birth of a child.

In the *Census Report for the Jaipur State* of 1903 there are illustrations
of designs for specific religious celebrations (7 & 8). The geomet-
rical diagrams have a quasi-magical quality; the stars, the sun, the
moon and the cosmos are also represented; and the most common
pattern is the lotus that symbolizes the goddess Devi or Lakshmi
who protects the home from evil spirits. Other images represent
the Creation – elephants, flowers, human figures. The floor patterns for different occasions used to be strictly followed, but now
the significance of the designs for each religious ceremony seems
only to be acknowledged in ashrams and temples.

6

A *kolam* or floor decoration at Sri Ramanasramam,
Tiruvannamalai, Tamil Nadu.

7 & 8

Designs (*chauk*) painted on the ground at the festivals
of Holi and Diwali, from the *Census Report for the Jaipur
State*, 1903. Courtesy Dr Y. Sahai.

Reed Mats and Tigerskins

The Indian love of decoration is also seen in floor-coverings.
In the thirteenth century, the coloured palm-leaf mats from
India's south-east coast were mentioned in travellers' accounts.[4]
Chatais, or floor mats, still found in practically every Indian
home, are a cheap alternative to other more labour-intensive
floor-coverings. Made of palm leaves, reeds, or other dried vegeta-
tion, they are cooler, more waterproof and more resistant to wear
and tear than carpets and cotton dhurries, and are sufficiently
flexible to be folded and stored on shelves.[5] Laid down for guests
to sit on at meal-times, during the monsoon they provide protection from the cold and often damp earthen floor. Laid on beds in
summer, they insulate from the heat.[6] They are also used as prayer
mats for Hindus (*asans*) and Muslims (*jainamaz*) in the home as
well as multi-niche prayer mats, or *safs*, in the mosques (*11*). The
patterns formed by the dyed strips on the neutral background are
often based on mud-floor paintings, using the same themes – the
Tree of Life, for instance, floral designs or abstract geometric patterns (*9*).[7] The composition, with central field and borders, is very
similar to a carpet design, with the same attention to detail.

Mats were greatly favoured for their coolness both by the
Indians and by the British (whose rule spread over almost all the
subcontinent from the late eighteenth century onwards). A watercolour painted by an Indian artist for Lady Impey, wife of the
British Governor of Bengal in the late eighteenth century, records
the Impey nursery with its striped Indian rush floor-covering
(*10*). The *sitalpatti* (cool matting) of Bengal, Assam and Tripura,
was woven on a loom with cotton warps for the finest and most
flexible mats.[8]

Tiger and leopard skins are shown as floor-coverings in Persian and Indian miniatures – exclusively for deities, rulers, ascetics and bards (*12*). In Buddhism as in Hinduism, the tiger symbolizes high rank, power and fearlessness.[9] In the Arabic fable book, *Kalila wa Dimna,* based on the Sanskrit version of the *Panchatantra,* the leopard sits in judgment over the jackal Dimna, showing the power of the lion-king vested in the leopard.[10] The god Shiva is often shown with a tiger or leopard skin (they seem to be interchangeable) representing the tiger killed by Shiva, showing that he is 'beyond the power of Nature. He is its master and carries the skin of the tiger as a trophy.'[11] In Hinduism tiger skins are often used as *asans,* prayer mats, as they are thought to be conducive to meditation and the channelling of higher energy. They also deter snakes, scorpions and insects, and are generally protective.

The History of the Dhurrie

The significance of animal skins and of ritual designs in floor paintings and mats also applies to the designs of dhurries. Like other Indian art forms, it assimilates new influences in its already extensive decorative vocabulary without losing its own identity. The charm of the dhurrie lies in the simple treatment of the decorative details, and the principles of symmetry and endless repetition. Although the dhurrie is occasionally made of wool, particularly in the north-west where it can be cold, it is generally

9

Below Bengali mat with a tree of life design.

10

Bottom left Impey nursery, watercolour, 1777–83, depicting rush floor-covering. Collection Impey family, Oxford.

11

Bottom right Detail of a multiniche prayer or *saf* reed mat in a mosque, Aurangabad, northern Deccan (Maharastra).

12

A musician playing bagpipes and a *chang* (harp), Mughal, *c.* 1590. The Nasser D. Khalili Collection of Islamic Art.

made of cotton. In most nineteenth-century records, the dhurrie is referred to as a *dari* or *satranji* in the north of India, and as a *jamkhani* in the south.[12]

The knotted carpet was probably introduced into India from Persia, but in the case of the dhurrie India had long had its own weaving industry, which was as renowned as its textile production. It is thought that the cotton rug fragment found by Sir Aurel Stein in 1901 at the ancient Niya site in Turkestan is Indian, and dated to the first to third centuries AD (*13*).[13] This fragment is now in the British Museum and may be the earliest surviving example of an Indian dhurrie. Trading between India and China via Central Asia was very active at this time. The pattern of stripes and alternating bands of *svastika*-type motifs, and the brilliant colour all support the Indian attribution. An analysis of the dyes, particularly the green, might be able to identify the plants used, which could confirm the Indian origin.

13

Opposite top Fragment of coloured rug from dwelling Niii, Niya Site, Turkestan. 24 x 47cm, 9½ x 18½ in. British Museum, London.

14

Opposite centre Prince Mahajanaka receiving a ceremonial bath, wallpainting, Ajanta Cave 1, *c.* 4th–6th centuries AD.

15

Opposite bottom Women sitting on striped cloth/dhurries, wallpainting, Ajanta Cave 1, *c.* 4th–6th centuries AD.

There are no other surviving dhurrie fragments from the period before the seventeenth century, and our knowledge of its history before this is confined to visual and literary sources. There are many reasons for this. The humble cotton flatweaves were not considered worth keeping, and the Indian climate is, moreover, not conducive to the preservation of delicate textiles. Floors should in principle be cleansed after meals, or if a person of low caste has stood or even cast a shadow on them, and this practice is connected with the ritual of destroying any sullied floor-coverings. Finally, the idea of a permanent floor-covering is contrary to Hindu belief – the floor decoration, which takes twenty-five minutes every day to paint, fades away within a couple of hours as people walk in and out of their dwellings.

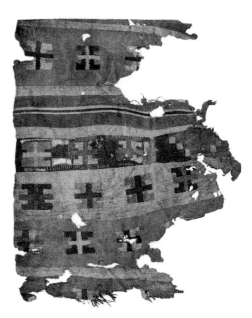

Possibly the earliest depiction of a dhurrie is to be seen in the Bhuddist paintings of the fourth to sixth centuries AD in the Ajanta Caves. In a scene from the *Mahajanaka Jataka* (in Cave 1),[14] some claim to see a plain dhurrie beneath the seated King Mahajanaka (*14*).[15] He is receiving a ceremonial bath before he renounces worldly things, however, so it is more likely that the dark blue with a red border is simply a basin. Although several other floor-coverings are depicted, some striped, it is not clear whether they are dhurries or not (see *15*).[16]

The earliest written mention of floor-coverings – dhurries or, more likely, rugs in general – is found in al-Maqdisi who wrote in the tenth century about the manufacture of *busut* (plural of *bsat*) in Sind. In classical Arabic, the word *bsat* refers to both knotted carpets and the humbler flatweave – *bsat* relates to *basit*, meaning humble, simple. In colloquial Arabic today, however, *bsat* refers only to a striped flatweave, or *kilim*.

Royal accounts and memoirs are a further source of written information on the dhurrie. The Mughal Empire was founded in India by Babur in 1526, and this Muslim dynasty was at its strongest and most magnificent in the sixteenth and seventeenth centuries. Deeply influenced by the Persian Safavid dynasty founded around 1502, the Mughal emperors and their nobles were great patrons of the arts, and Persian was the language spoken at court. In the *Ain-i Akbari,* the account of the reign of Akbar the Great (1556–1605), there are references to the production of

The Patriarch Abraham Plays Host to a Fire Worshipper,
miniature from the *Bustan* of Sa'di, Sultanate,
Mandu *c.* 1500–03. National Museum, New Delhi.

flatweaves, *satranji,* in the late sixteenth century in the royal workshops of Lahore, Agra and Fatehpur Sikri — knotted carpets are
mentioned with '*jajams, shatranjis* and *baluchis*'. It is thought that
satranji derives from *shatranj,* the Persian word for the game of
chess, but a more plausible explanation is that *satranji,* a Hindustani word, comes from the Hindu *sat* meaning seven and the
Persian *rang* meaning colour.

As for the many paintings of dhurries, one of the very earliest
depictions of a striped dhurrie is to be seen in a miniature from
the *Bustan* of Sa'di, *c.* 1500, from the pre-Mughal Sultanate period,
when most of the subcontinent was under the rule of indepen-
dent Muslim states. Abraham and his guest are sitting on an
elaborate carpet with a Kufic border, and their food is displayed
on a striped pale blue and indigo dhurrie (*16*).

There are also early paintings of the dhurrie in the
manuscript of the *Padshahnama* and related works of the 1630s and
1640s. In a miniature from the St Petersburg Album, *Shah Jahan in*

17

A Night Celebrating the Prophet's Birthday, Agra Diwan-i 'Amm, September 1633, attributed to Bulaqui, son of Hoshang, *c.* 1635. Courtesy Freer Gallery of Art, Washington, DC.

Darbar, c. 1630, there is a striped dhurrie in the foreground. *A Night Celebrating the Prophet's Birthday, Agra, c.* 1635 (*17*), now in the Freer Gallery of Art, Washington, DC, shows steps covered with a striped dhurrie. In another miniature, *Shah Jahan Honouring his Son Prince Aurangzeb at Agra before his Wedding* (from the *Padshahnama, c.* 1640), the steps on which Aurangzeb stands are covered with a striped dhurrie.[17]

Although any floor-covering with a striped pattern depicted in a painting is almost certainly a dhurrie, we can only speculate about many of the more elaborate designs. Dhurries were certainly in use in the seventeenth century in the spring and summer when a knotted carpet would be too warm, but dhurrie designs are so similar to Mughal carpets that it is difficult to tell from a painting whether they are carpets or dhurries.

The earliest and most unimpeachable evidence we have of an Indian flat woven rug is now in the Calico Museum of Textiles in Ahmedabad, Gujarat (*18*),[18] and was originally in the Amber

Palace in Rajasthan. It has a cotton warp, but woollen wefts, and is known to have been woven around the middle of the seventeenth century in Lahore. In the prison workshop in Lahore today they are still producing dhurries with a cotton warp and woollen wefts, a floor-covering suitable for the cold winters of the Punjab. Other fragments, one with a tiger motif, are in the same museum.

Another dhurrie dating from the same period also exists now only as a fragment (19). I rediscovered it in the Bharat Kala Bhavan Museum in Benares (Varanasi).[19] It was wrapped in an old carpet and was an anonymous gift to the museum; it has never been published, and had been forgotten. The design is typical of the mid- to late seventeenth-century Mughal Lahore-type dhurrie with cotton warp and woollen weft in the characteristic flat woven and interlocking technique. The indigo ground has alternating cypress trees, and stylized poppies or tulips in a vase. The border has a similar alternating design of a cypress tree with stylized flower buds in a vase, and the outer border has an indigo cross motif alternating with a rosette within red and green stripe and a red skirt. The colour scheme – indigo, red, green, yellow and pinks – is also typical of Mughal designs in general, and the borders found in both dhurries are very similar to those of vase carpets from Kerman in Persia, which was on the great caravan route to India. Kerman province under Safavid rule had a close relationship with India, and there is much written evidence of carpets being exported to India at the time of Akbar the Great.

Travellers' accounts are valuable in giving a picture of life in the Mughal court, and there are descriptions by Dutch, Portuguese and English observers, but it is difficult to know whether they are writing of dhurries or carpets. Most Europeans could not tell the difference between them, clearly seen in the Reverend Terry's remark in 1655: 'They make likewise excellent carpets of

18

Above Mughal flatweave, Lahore, *c.* 1640–50. 3.73 x 10.06m, 11ft 4¾in x 33ft. Calico Museum, Ahmedabad.

19

Right Fragment of a Mughal flatweave, Probably Lahore, mid 17th century. 2.34 x 0.43m, 7ft 8in x 1ft 5in. Bharat Kalat Bhavan Museum, Varanasi.

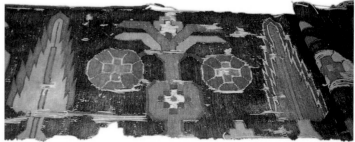

their cotton wool.'[20] It was only in the early years of the nineteenth century that the distinction was better understood, and at the time of the 1851 Great Exhibition in London, where dhurries and carpets were on display side by side, the difference was generally accepted. The Dutch traveller John Huyghen van Linscoten, however, in his 1598 memoirs, was the exception in his attempts to differentiate between the knotted carpet and what appears to be striped cotton rugs: 'They make likewise many carpets, called Alcatiffas…and another sort of coarse carpets that are called Banquays, which are much like the striped Coverlets that are made in Scotland….'[21]

After the 'grand' dhurries of the seventeenth century, there are practically no known dhurries surviving apart from a few dubious fragments in private collections. The most intriguing and earliest dateable example comes from the Nizam of Hyderabad's royal workshop, or *karkhana* (20). It is a sample, never published before, with a pink and natural striped design and a stepped ending to the stripe, typical of the Deccan. It is stamped with three round seals inscribed in Persian. Unfortunately the seals are too faded to be clearly read, but the words 'servant of…Shah, 1107' can just be deciphered. The Hijra date of 1107 (AD 1695–96) corresponds to the reign of the Mughal ruler Aurangzeb (1658–1707). Round seals in *nasta'liq* script (a typical Persian script) without any division or decoration do not in any event post-date Aurangzeb's era. Manijeh Bayani associates the round seal with a dignitary connected with the Mughal court, which accords with the fact that it came from the Nizam's household.[22] The other inscriptions on the sample are legible: an inventory number of 1801; most important is 'private apartment', meaning ladies' quarters. This sample survived because, belonging to a private royal workshop, it was kept in the palace archives.

By the early nineteenth century, British rule extended over practically the whole of the subcontinent, and British administrators began their meticulous recording of the details of crafts and industrial products. In this century, dhurrie manufacturing entered a new and highly organized phase, which led to several exhibitions of dhurries in Europe and India. This coincided with

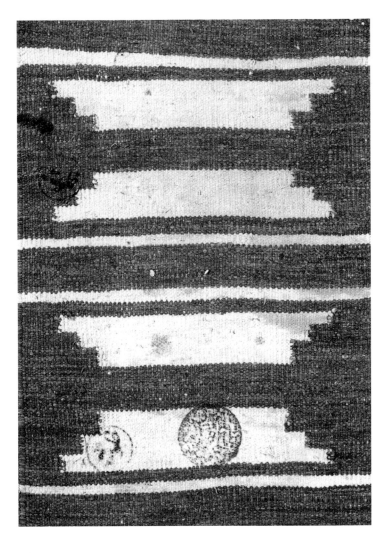

20

Detail of the pink and natural striped dhurrie sample from the Nizam of Hyderabad's *karkhana*, *c.* 1700. Private collection.

Inscriptions on the dhurrie sample (20)

'1801' [inventory no?]	١٨٠١
'2 dhir'a and 6' [??]	٢ نرعه ٦ //
'14 knots' [*girih* also means ⅙ of *gas* or yard, three fingerbreadths]	١٤ گره
'Total, one' [item]	جمع ايك عدد
'41' [??]	(٤١)
'Private apartment'	خلوت

The round seal impression:

بنده (؟) ... شين شاه ١١٥٧ (؟)

'The servant of [?]…shin shah 1157 [1744–5 ?]'

the finest and most creative period of cotton dhurrie weaving in India, lasting approximately eighty years. It started in 1851 with the Great Exhibition at Crystal Palace, London – the first major industrial exhibition in Europe to promote international trade and manufacture – a 'tile' design dhurrie was used as the backdrop of the Indian Pavilion (*21*). Similar exhibitions in India followed to promote the crafts of different provinces. This highly productive period lasted until the late 1930s when Bikaner Central Jail won the All India Hand Weaving and Printing Competition 1936–37, awarded by the Government of the United Provinces.

Dhurrie-weaving was divided into two organized sectors, a private industry and a prison industry. There was also the third important sector of village production. In the private industry, well organized and commercially successful workshops were set up in towns, and sample books and proper labelling were introduced (see *22–25*). This commercial sector was led by the cotton mills, generally British owned, such as Muir Mills in Cawnpore (now Kanpur), in the United Provinces. In the *Imperial Gazetteer of India, Provincial Series*, the section on commerce in Rajputana

21
Coloured engraving of the Indian Pavilion, Great Exhibition, Crystal Palace, London, 1851, with tile dhurrie backdrop.

(Rajasthan) in 1908 describes Krishna Cotton Mill in Kishangarh and Beawar near Ajmer.[23] The reputation of the mills was such that their striped dhurries were found all over India. There is a striped dhurrie from Muir Mills, for example, in Darbargadh Palace in Morvi, in the state of Gujarat (24). There may have been pressure from the British Resident to purchase goods from British-owned mills.

The workshops in Agra, an old dhurrie-weaving centre, go back to the reign of Akbar when dhurries were woven alongside Agra's famous carpets, and also now provided standard designs. Production here concentrated mainly on striped and multi-niche prayer dhurries (safs). The dhurrie illustrated (23) was being cleaned with other safs in the laundry section of the Central Jail in Baroda (Vadodara) and came from a local mosque.

In the nineteenth and early twentieth centuries many monographs were written about the arts and crafts of India. T. N. Mukharji, in his work of 1888 on dhurrie production, does not mention the mills, which produced large quantities of 'run-of-the-mill' dhurries.[24] He focused instead on the centres of Indian-run industry. The British records tended to stress either British-owned or British 'encouraged' industries in the mills and jails; the Indian monographs concentrated on locally owned industries and workshops.

In The Industrial Arts of India published in 1880, Sir George Birdwood describes cotton production state by state, but when it comes to dhurries his comments lack precision. On Rajasthan he mentions the large cotton dhurries striped in red, green, yellow, blue and black, and marvels at the skill of the weavers at 'harmonizing the most prismatic colours'.[25] He describes the production in Adoni, Madras district (Andhra Pradesh) of large cotton carpets, most probably dhurries, for houses and tents, and of a smaller size for Indian troops (probably used for bedding).

22

Top Label from an Agra commercial workshop, *c.* 1920.

23

Centre Back of a multi-niche prayer dhurrie or *saf* stamped '14M Produce of Agra', *c.* 1910.

24

Above Label of the Muir Mills, Cawnpore, late 19th century, Darbargadh Palace, Morvi.

25

Left Sample book from Agra, *c.* 1930. T. C. Goel/ Samurai Collection.

He also mentions that these 'carpets' were exported in large quantities to all parts of southern India.[26] He specifically mentions the striped cotton carpets, *'daris'* or *'satrangis'* of the Kolar district and at Shikarpur, in the Shimoga district (both in the southern state of Karnataka),[27] and seems to equate the striped dhurries with *'daris'* or *'satrangis'*, referring to all other cotton dhurries as carpets. Furthermore he reports that 'the striped *satrangis* of very superior texture are made at Rangpur (Bengal)'.[28] N. G. Mukerji, however, in his monograph on the carpet industry in Bengal in 1907, does not refer to the production in Rangpur.[29] Like the mills, the production at Rangpur may have been British-supported. In general, south Indian dhurrie-weaving is the least well known – the climate did not necessitate large-scale use of cotton dhurries indoors. Functional rather than decorative, dhurries here were mainly striped and used for bedding, tents and religious gatherings, such as festivals and prayers.

Dhurries from the Deccan already had a very high reputation. They benefited from the sophisticated designs of the Deccan's famous carpets, and elaborate patterned dhurries were the fashion in the home.

The weaving industry in the north east, as at Patna in the state of Bihar, was also very highly regarded. In his voluminous

26

Musicians and a nautch dancer perform on a striped dhurrie, 19th-century photograph. India Office Library, London.

work on the textile fabrics of India, *Textile Manufactures of the People of India and their Costumes* (1886), W. Forbes-Watson provides actual samples of dhurries from the subcontinent, and itemizes dimensions, weight, price and region: 'India Fabrics no. 435... Cotton 'Suttringee' or rug. From Mangalore: Madras. Length 1 yard 32 inches. Width 32 inches. Weight 2lbs 4oz. Price 3s.' Beside it was glued a sample of this striped dhurrie (27).

Despite the interest in cotton production and dhurrie-weaving, none of the monographs or articles gives a detailed description of the designs or techniques used. It seems that the local workshops or mills concentrated on standard plain designs for a mass market.

Prison Workshops

The private industries competed fiercely with the prison workshops. The leap from a small industry catering to local needs and from royal *karkhanas* (workshops) to aggressive commercial ventures, led to rivalry between jails — where time and turnover were not an issue — and commercial workshops — where profit was paramount. The private sector tried to discredit the prison workshops by accusing them of producing poor quality carpets and dhurries.

Prison weaving workshops were included among many of the reforms and enlightened enterprises pioneered by the maharajas of India. The move from royal workshop to prison workshop was led by the Maharaja of Jaipur, Sawai Ram Singh II, who, it is claimed, was the first to set up a weaving workshop. He built a new jail in Jaipur in 1856 and introduced reforms to improve the conditions of the prisoners,[30] and he also introduced the idea of employing prisoners. By teaching them a skill, the prison gave them a chance to participate positively in the life of the jail, and a means of earning a living on release.

The industries carried on in the jails also had a second aim, namely to make the prisons as economically viable as possible, and sometimes even profitable. This practice is still followed in both India and Pakistan. In the fifteen jails in India and five jails in Pakistan that I visited, the prisoners are still employed and sometimes paid (in 1998 around Indian Rs 300 per

27
'Striped dhurrie sample from Mangalore: Madras.' From *Textile Manufactures of the People of India and their Costumes* by W. Forbes-Watson, 1886, Vol. VII. Courtesy Lahore Museum.

month for a weaver for eight hours a day) to work at furniture-making, weaving, dyeing, paper- and soap-making. The weavers usually work in partly shaded courtyards where a master weaver, normally a jail employee and not a fellow inmate, oversees the production.

Dhurrie-weaving is only taught in jails to prisoners serving life or long-term sentences – a minimum of five years is necessary to make economic sense for the jail to invest in teaching a prisoner the skill. In the prisons I visited, it takes six months to teach a prisoner to weave, and eighteen months for him to reach an adequately competent level. The most skilled weaver I met was in Jodhpur high-security jail – he had been imprisoned for seventeen years. He was weaving an intricate dhurrie from a photograph in a book (28). Weaving is still considered a man's job, and is only taught to male prisoners.

Most jail weavers worked from sample rolls, with sometimes as many as twenty different patterns in a roll. The sample designs are approximately 45cm (18in) square, showing a central field and a border, and given a number for identification. Rolls also had a series of stripes in different colour combinations, or plain fields with contrasting borders. The individual who commissioned the dhurrie would point out a particular design, quote its number and perhaps change the colours or border. Many jails, however, just kept fragments or small-format dhurries as references. They are an invaluable part of the history of dhurrie-weaving, as they indicate the abundance and provenance of designs.

Exhibition catalogues, such as that for the Delhi exhibition of 1902–03 by George Watt, or publications like H. J. R. Twigg's 1907

28
Dhurrie weaving from a design found in a book, Jodhpur Central Jail.

monograph on carpets in the Bombay Presidency, are useful in helping us to identify the designs illustrated, but attribution remains difficult. Most jails produced sample rolls with standard designs and standard borders. The reason for this was that the master weavers or overseers were appointed in one jail and were then posted to another, taking the designs with them. In 1868, for instance, a Mr Williams, formerly an overseer at Agra jail, was appointed to organize the industrial departments of Jaipur jail, and set up weaving workshops.[31] The same samples were therefore used from jail to jail up and down the country.

If the technical information necessary to identify original work from a particular prison was available, there would be less confusion. Most jails used, and still use, different types of cotton yarn, nowadays machine-spun. The technical analysis of a sample could help identify the type of yarn used by a particular jail. This would only apply to standard dhurries, however, and even so there seem to be no rules these days regarding yarns for standard dhurries – jails within the same state use different yarns. For special commissions, furthermore, the commissioner generally provided his own yarn, probably handspun, dyed with natural dyes and of high quality. Identification of dhurries is based mainly on provenance, as technical analysis and design are not necessarily conclusive.

Aurangabad, previously in northern Deccan and now in Maharashtra, has a jail within the city walls. The jail provided the local Chishti shrine (dating from the early seventeenth century) and adjoining mosque with prayer rugs. The Waqf (Islamic Endowment Board) ordered three *safs* from the jail fifty years ago. In this shrine there are *safs* with the thin stripe repeat design that was particular to a Chishti place of worship – this will be discussed further in Chapters 1 and 6.

The weaving workshop in Jaipur Jail, attributed to the pioneering reforms of the Maharaja of Jaipur, held a rare copy of T. H. Hendley's book *Asian Carpets*, with plates of Jaipur's famous carpet collection, mostly Persian, Turkish and Central Asian designs. Prisoners could use this as patterns for designs.[32] In his *Notes on Jaipur*, published in 1909, Lt Colonel H. L. Showers describes both the central and district jail, and is very informative

29

Weavers working on a horizontal loom, Jodhpur Central Jail.

Lord Curzon (Viceroy of India 1898–1905) and other dignitaries standing on striped dhurries, from an album of old photographs, *c.* 1900. Courtesy Mehra Fine Arts, New Delhi.

on the jail industries. 'The carpet industry has obtained a high degree of excellence and the carpets turned out here are much in demand both in India, in Europe and in America. Persian, Turkish and Central Asian designs are copied.'[33] He describes the cotton dhurries as being 'of excellent quality and design, they are priced at Rs 1-8-o to Rs 7. a square yard according to quality.'[34] The cost of purchase was just above that of the material used, which made them an attractive buy.[35] Quality depended on who commissioned the dhurrie – the Maharaja or the Viceroy would certainly have received the best (30) – and the master weaver. There was always a danger, however, in being labelled an outstandingly good weaver – it meant that the prisoner was less likely to be released on the Maharaja's birthday.[36]

Jaipur Jail supplied carpets to the *diwan-i khas* (hall of audience), both of the City Palace and the Rambagh Palace. Lt Colonel J. P. Huban, Inspector General of Jails, Jaipur State, notes 'that a number of dhurries now in use in the Viceroy's house, New Delhi, were manufactured in this factory',[37] and that Lord Irwin (Viceroy of India 1926–31 and later Lord Halifax), the Commander-in-Chief and other notables also purchased Jaipur dhurries to take back to England.[38] In 1996 when I visited the Central Jail, there were several samples on the walls and sample rolls in the depot. I photographed about twenty of the earlier samples, which included patterned, striped and prayer dhurries.

The Bikaner City Jail (Rajasthan) was built in 1872 by Maharaja Dungar Singh. Bikaner was already known for the quality of its wool, and its jail carpet industry flourished in the nineteenth century to reach its all-time peak in the early twentieth century. According to the *Report on the Administration of the Bikanir State for 1893–94*,[39] shown to me among the jail archives, the workshop was set up in 1885–86. Dhurrie production grew alongside the carpet industry and benefited from the skill and creativity of its master weavers. The jail was awarded seventeen medals between 1900 and 1937 for its carpets and dhurries, including the bronze medal awarded by the French Republic to '*Son Altesse Le Maharajah de Bikaner*' at the Exposition Universelle of 1900 and a medal from the India Art Exhibition, Delhi, 1902–03; in the official catalogue Watt illustrates a Bikaner dhurrie of floral and animal pattern.[40] Also noteworthy is the gold medal awarded to Bikaner State at the Festival of Empire, Imperial Exhibition and Pageant of London, Crystal Palace, 1911.

Both carpets and dhurries are still woven in Bikaner Central Jail, contrary to reports,[41] and the prisoners are very proud of their skills. There is currently an attempt to save the magnificent horizontal large looms (34), over a hundred years old, as the jail is to be relocated outside the city. Bikaner also has an archive of dhurrie samples and fragments larger than any I have seen in India

31 & 32

A selection of dhurrie samples at Bikaner Central Jail, which keeps one of the largest dhurrie sample archives in the subcontinent.

Dhurrie sample with elephant and figures, c. 1930, Udaipur Jail.

and Pakistan. I personally photographed and catalogued over eighty pieces (*31 & 32*). Among the archives were two books on dyeing: *A Catalogue for Organic and Inorganic Laboratory Chemicals*, ICI India Ltd, 1961, and *I. G. Farben Industrie*, Aktiengesellshaft. Unfortunately both were in poor condition.

Jodhpur Jail (Rajasthan) was built in 1894–95, and housed a local dhurrie industry that catered mainly for the Maharaja of Jodhpur. Spinning, and vegetable and chemical dyeing were also carried out here and still are. Jodhpur had among its archives a woven map of India before Independence in 1947, a couple of long sample rolls and a few samples.

Udaipur Jail, a small Rajasthani prison and originally a Jaipur sub-jail, was built about a hundred years ago. It did not have a carpet industry in the nineteenth century,[42] but dhurrie-weaving was introduced in the first part of the twentieth century, and is still practised. Dyeing is also done on the premises, but only with

100-year-old horizontal loom in Bikaner Central Jail.

chemical dyes. It has a small selection of samples and sample rolls, about twenty-eight in total, and the designs are similar to those of Bikaner and Jaipur jails. According to the master weaver I met in 1997, the samples in the jail were fifty to sixty years old, and included striped, Tree of Life and geometric patterns and a small sample with little figures and elephants (33).

Baroda Jail (Vadodara, Gujarat), built in 1881 by the Maharaja Sayajirao Gaikwad, is one of the most thriving jails in India. The weaving section is extensive, and the spinning of cotton is all done in the jail. Sadly, it has disposed of its dhurrie samples, as storage problems mean that archives are destroyed every ten years. In the laundry section of the jail, however, I found some interesting old *safs* from a local mosque being washed (23).

Sabarmati Jail (Ahmedabad, Gujarat) has the best collection of dhurrie sample rolls (36) after Bikaner, and also a Noah's Ark dhurrie (35). The jail still has a thriving dhurrie-weaving industry (contrary to other reports).[43] The jail was built 1894–96, and the yarns, which are machine-spun, are purchased already dyed. Large horizontal looms are favoured.

Yeravda Jail, Poona (Pune, Maharastra) was built in 1861 by the British. Its highly organized weaving industry was set up in 1875. It was famous for its carpets and dhurrie production, and its sample collection was extensive, as reported by George Watt in 1902 and Steven Cohen in *The Unappreciated Dhurrie* eighty years later. Some early Scrolling Leaves and Blossom carpet fragments cover the jail superintendent's office floor. The jail's products attracted notice at the India Art Exhibition in Delhi 1902–03. The workshop uses small vertical looms, pit-looms and large vertical looms (see pp. 34–36). Of its horizontal looms, only three are now in operation, as demand for large dhurries is limited.

Hyderabad Jail (Andhra Pradesh) was built in 1876 by the Nizam of Hyderabad. Dhurrie-weaving is now mainly concentrated in Warangal Jail (Andhra Pradesh). When I visited the Jami Masjid in Hyderabad and asked to see the *farrashkhana* (warehouse) where the multi-niche prayer dhurries are kept, one of the keepers showing me the *safs* told me that his father, now retired, had been the master weaver at Hyderabad jail, and remembers the Islamic Endowment Board placing an order, forty years ago, for dhurries

35

Top Noah's Ark dhurrie, inscribed 'A.C.P. 1915', for 'Ahmedabad Central Prison', Sabarmati Central Jail.

36

Above Dhurrie sample roll, *c.* 1900, Sabarmati Central Jail, Ahmedabad.

37
A display of dhurries and carpets in Lucknow Central
Jail Shop, *c.* 1950. Photo courtesy Lucknow Central Jail.

for the mosque. The designs were based on samples of old *safs*
provided by the mosque.

Agra Jail (Uttar Pradesh) was known for its carpets and dhurries in the early twentieth century. All of its archives were disposed
of when it was rebuilt around 1990. According to the super-inten-
dent, the dhurrie samples were sent to Lucknow Jail depot.

Lucknow Jail (Uttar Pradesh) was built 1860–70. According
to its superintendent, the weaving of floral and elaborate
dhurries (see 37) stopped around 1987. In the depot I found only
four samples, none of any consequence. According to Steven
Cohen in *The Unappreciated Dhurrie*, there were several interesting
dhurrie samples here in the early 1980s. They have now disappeared, and there was also no trace of the Agra jail samples.

Multan Jail in western Punjab (now in Pakistan) first built in
1873, was rebuilt after being destroyed by floods in 1930. Multan
produces some of the finest cotton in the region, and some of the
finest dhurries came from here — the Victoria and Albert Museum
in London has two geometric dhurries purchased directly from
the jail in the nineteenth century. The jail has a few samples that

38
A cartoon of a dhurrie pattern, used as a guide
for weaving. Lahore Jail, Pakistan.

are about fifty years old, most of which use chemically dyed yarn, and the jail does its own chemical dyeing.

Bahawalpur Jail, in western Punjab (now in Pakistan), a few hours' drive from Multan, also has a fine dhurrie industry. The old central jail, originally built by the Maharaja of Bahawalpur, was rebuilt after the floods of 1930. Spinning and dyeing is done on the premises. The prisoners do not receive a salary but have five to eight days' remission a month, unless the commission is private, in which case they are paid a little. The jail possesses a couple of samples, and mainly horizontal looms, both large and small. The small looms are the standard bed dhurrie size, that is, approximately 1.2 x 1.8 metres (4 x 6 feet). The weaving is carried out in small sheds or workshops, each with its own master weaver.

Lahore Jail, the largest in the Punjab (and now in Pakistan), has a thriving carpet- and dhurrie-weaving output. The weavers produce dhurries alongside carpets, and benefit from the designs and master weavers. As in Multan and Bahawalpur jails, the weavers work from a *talim* (a numbered card) and sometimes also a cartoon of the pattern (38). It is the only jail where I saw woollen dhurries being made with a cotton warp and a woollen weft. The wool is bought and dyed outside the jail.

Hyderabad Jail (Sindh, Pakistan), built in 1894, one of the oldest jails, has only a section of an early sample roll, showing a plain field and a key border in terracotta and blue vegetable dyes.

39
A multi-niche prayer dhurrie or *saf* being woven in Multan Jail, Pakistan.

Village Production

Dhurrie-weaving plays an important part in the life of village women. As with floor paintings, the tradition is passed on from mother to daughter. Geometric patterns, stylized birds and plant motifs all have a particular significance, and form a major part of this decorative vocabulary.

Dhurries are generally made for personal use, or as dowries and gifts. The dowry, still very important in this part of the world, was also a way of handing down designs and techniques. Ann Shankar and Jenny Housego devoted *Bridal Durries of India* (1996) to a study of the current production in northern India, mainly in the former state of eastern Punjab.

A girl normally starts preparing for her dowry at ten years old, and most of her mother's free time is also spent on it. The patterns are often traditional and represent auspicious symbols of fertility, prosperity and protection from destructive forces or deities. Hindu communities tend to draw on naturalistic motifs such as flowers and birds, particularly peacocks; Muslim communities favour geometric, small and symmetrical patterns in keeping with the strict rules of non-representation that Islam dictates. The dhurries are mainly for the home — floor-coverings or part of the bedding. They are woven on a small loom, which takes up little precious space and is easy to set up and dismantle.

The cotton is generally handspun by the women, but the yarns are sent to a nearby town or village to be dyed professionally by the men. Dyeing was and still is a secretive profession. The dyers, from the same caste and often from the same family, pass the vegetable and mineral recipes only from master to apprentice.

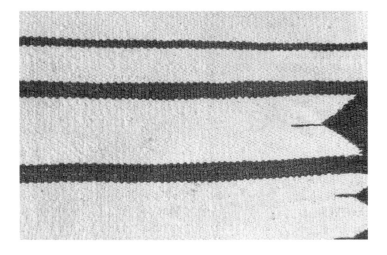

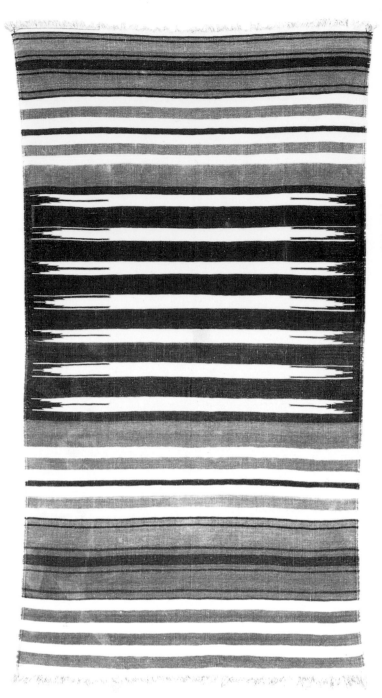

40

Above Village striped dhurrie with *ikat* motif, Kutch, Gujarat, *c.* 1880. 1.07 x 1.98m, 3ft 6in x 6ft 6in. T. C. Goel/ Samurai Collection.

41

Left Detail of a village striped dhurrie with handspun cotton, loose weave and natural dyes, Rajasthan, *c.* 1880.

42

Opposite above Dhurrie, Bhuj, Kutch, Gujarat, *c.* 1910, 2.06 x 3.96m, 6ft 9in x 13ft. T. C. Goel/Samurai Collection.

43

Opposite below Detail of *durbar* scene, wallpainting, early 19th century, Durbar Hall, Juna Mahal, Dungarpur, Rajasthan.

On special occasions, or for commission, women would weave large dhurries for a local temple or a wealthy landlord, a striped design or a simple geometric pattern. Village dhurries are easy to recognize, as they have a certain folk quality, and are generally loosely woven and made of handspun cotton (41).

Materials and Techniques

Weaving in India is often alluded to in the Vedas (the ancient sacred scriptures). As we have seen in the Ajanta cave paintings, coloured stripes were probably among the most ancient form of ornamentation once the art of plain weaving had been mastered.

According to Strabo, when Alexander the Great arrived in India in 327 BC, the Greeks noticed that the people wore garments made of 'tree wool' or 'wool produced in nuts'.[44] Cotton, which is native to India, was cheaper and cooler than wool, and its availability and strength made it a favourite with weavers, for it provided sturdy warps (the basic structure of a woven fabric) even when a carpet or a dhurrie was made of wool. It kept its shape when woven, and could be very finely spun and woven – the prayer dhurrie of the Nizam Of Hyderabad (228) was so finely woven it almost felt like silk.

Legend has it that a princess hid a couple of silkworm cocoons in her headdress when she left China to be married to an Indian king in the fifth century AD. Silk is extensively cultivated in India, and is still equated with wealth and status. Widely used in Kashmir carpets, in dhurries it is mainly found as a decorative feature, usually for dowry dhurries or rulers' ceremonial dhurries. In south India, where the silk saris are famous, finely woven cotton striped dhurries occasionally have a couple of fine silk stripes in contrasting colours, top and bottom. Silver and gold, or other metal threads are also used, often in combination with silk, for such ceremonial dhurries as the indigo and white dhurrie (42) with Tree of Life motifs, yellow and pink *mahi* or fish, and feathered diamonds of pink silk thread, silver and silver-gilt.

In the northern regions of India and in Pakistan, the climate requires warmer floor-coverings, and the influence of the woollen flatweaves and artefacts of adjacent nomadic tribes (such as the Baluchis in Pakistan) has led to woollen dhurries being made, but

production is dwindling – the woollen dhurrie is made mainly for export and on a small scale by comparison with Indian carpets. The fashion for wool carpets (mainly copies of traditional Persian designs), and their wide availability in India and Pakistan make them the preferred choice of floor-covering.

Originally camelhair was used for its strength as reinforcement and for insulating qualities superior to those of sheep wool. Camel or goat hair is occasionally included now as a decorative feature, particularly in the region of Kutch in Gujarat.

Spinning

In all communities, cotton was originally handspun with a *charka* wheel, a wooden spinning wheel. In India both men and women did the spinning, as it was laborious and time-consuming. For that reason, machine-spun cotton is now preferred, and is supplied by the numerous power mills in India, particularly those of Bombay (Mumbai) and Ahmedabad. Although ready-bleached cotton yarn is still dyed in some jails, the spinning-wheel is now mainly used to wind bobbins with different coloured yarns.

In rural areas, small villages in particular, in both India and Pakistan, women and young girls spin in their spare time. Handspun cotton has flexible and elastic properties that machine-spun cotton cannot achieve. An attempt to encourage hand-spinning is now practised in some cottage industries in northern India, particularly in the states of Gujarat, Rajasthan and Uttar Pradesh.

Spinning twists the cotton fibres either in a clockwise direction, referred to as a Z twist, or an anti-clockwise direction, known as S twist. Two or more threads are spun together for strength to form a plied yarn. For large cotton dhurries, the yarn used is multi-ply, as great strength is required for long warps. The yarn is normally twisted in a direction opposite to that of the threads to prevent unravelling, and is classified according to the direction of the twist of the threads, the number of threads used in the ply and then by the direction of the twist of the ply. In Sabarmati jail, Ahmedabad, for instance, the current combination used for the warp is Z4S or Z6S and for the weft Z6S. Most sale catalogues nowadays give this vital information.

Dyeing

India has long been known for its dyes and their fastness. The Persians and Greeks had a great appreciation of Indian textiles because of their unique use of brilliant colours.[45] As early as the third millennium BC, woven textiles and natural dyes were among India's greatest assets and exports, and the knowledge of how to fix a dye on cloth was one of India's greatest skills. At Mohenjo-daro, a third-millennium BC archaeological site on the Indus river in present-day Pakistan, fragments of red woven textiles were found wrapped around a silver pot. The madder dye requires a mordant to fix the colour, and the presence of dye vats at the site indicate a relatively advanced knowledge of the dyeing processes.[46]

Hinduism has always attached a cosmological importance to colours and, as with gemstones, each planet was represented by a

45
Indigo dyeing in Sitapur, Uttar Pradesh.

colour: for instance, black cloth is a reference to Saturn, red to Mars and yellow to Venus.[47] Poetry, colour and music are also closely connected in Hindu culture. Mood, tones and hues are almost interchangeable. The word *raga*, used in traditional Indian music, indicates both a mood in music and also a dye. From the simple pale indigo and natural stripe to the more elaborate combinations from opposite ends of the spectrum, the success of a dhurrie depends on the delicate balance between colour and design. The natural colour (almost white) of the ready-bleached cotton yarn is used extensively, because it contributes to the overall light effect, essential in hot climates, and, since no dyeing process is involved, is also cheaper. It is often used with indigos, terracottas or pinks in large festival or tent dhurries.

The most attractive colours come from natural dyes, and are subtle, combine harmoniously with each other and fade evenly when exposed to light, lasting longer than chemical dyes. The natural dyeing process, whether animal, vegetable or mineral, was and still is a well kept secret in India, although in the seventeenth century European traders discovered some recipes. The *abrash*, or variation in the same colour, which occasionally appears and contributes greatly to the character of the dhurrie, is caused by dyeing the batches of cotton yarns separately – the temperature and the length of immersion affect the intensity of colour, and the recipes are never precise. The quality of the natural dyes depends on the quality of the river water, and long exposure to the sun in drying.

46

Drying the yarn after dyeing, Sanganer, Rajasthan.

Indigo, walnut husks and certain leaves are the only natural dyes that do not require a mordant to fix the colour in the fibre. For the rest, alum is the most commonly used, but different mordants are used for different fibres.

Indigo or *nila*, comes from the indigo shrub (*Indigofera tinctoria*), mainly from the leaves. These are immersed in a vat with an alkaline liquid (urine is often used) to make the brew in which the yarn is steeped. Skilful timing was vital to obtain the depth of blue required. Indigo is extremely fast even when exposed to light.

A widely used crimson-red cotton dye is extracted from the root of the *chay* plant (*Oldenlandia umbellata*) which grows on the Coromandel coast in south India. Calcium is an essential component of the dyeing process. Madder was introduced to western India in the late eighteenth century by the East India Company. The madder plant (*Rubia tinctoria*) produces red dyes that vary from red when the mordant is alum to violet when the mordant is pure iron. It is reasonably fast when exposed to light. *Manjeet*, a plant from the madder family, yielded a crimson red widely used in western India where it was cultivated around Bombay region. *Saranguy*, also known as *āl*, from the young cultivated roots of the *Morinda citrifolia* tree, yields a brick-red colour used in northern and western India.

Lac (*Taccifer lacca*) is a pink pigment from the female lac insect. It is expensive because thousands of insects have to be collected for the resinous deposit. It is used mainly in silk dyeing, and can be found in silk inclusions in dowry dhurries or in specially commissioned dhurries.

Turmeric (*Curcuma Longa*), also known as *haldi* or *haridra* in India, is a tuber which yields a deep yellow fast dye on cotton. Indigo and turmeric were used in succession to produce a green that was fast on cotton. A whole range of colours could be created by combining other plants and insects and minerals.

Synthetic dyes were introduced in India in the 1880s. The new dyes, essentially chemical compounds, were cheaper than the natural dyes and easier to use. They did not require a mordant, or a time-consuming process, and yielded bright and consistent colours. Synthetic indigo replaced the expensive natural dye so accurately that it ruined the indigo industry. Needless to say, the

47

Vertical loom, Bikaner Central Jail, Rajasthan.

Pit-loom, Yeravda Central Jail, Pune. A pit is dug out of the earth for the loom, and the weaver sits on the edge of the pit.

jails were among the first to adopt synthetic dyes as they were cost effective. The only exception was Yeravda Jail in Pune which prided itself on the quality of its dyeing and weaving. According to Birdwood, the devastating effect that these new dyes had on the local economy led the Maharaja of Kashmir to adopt extreme measures — any magenta dyes that were not confiscated or destroyed were subject to a heavy import duty.[48]

India, long famed for its natural dyeing, lost this ancient and precious craft. Chemical dyeing, however, produces harsh and strident colours. Only since the 1990s, and mainly through Western demand, have attempts been made to reintroduce natural dyeing by craftsmen.

Colour and dyes help to date and identify a dhurrie. Natural colours often use indigenous dyestuff which on occasions can indicate the region in which it was woven. Madder was mainly used in western India, for instance, while a red from the *chay* plant originates from the Coromandel coast. But dyestuff was in great demand, so it also travelled, hence the abundant use of indigo. Synthetic oranges and bright greens appear from the late nineteenth century in dhurries all over India, and are easy to recognize by the striking contrast with the mellow tone of the natural dye.

The Loom

There has been very little change over the centuries in the process of weaving a dhurrie. Three different types of looms are used. The most common is the standard horizontal hand loom, favoured in jails and workshops; smaller versions were used in village production. In jail workshops the horizontal loom is operated with up to seven prisoners in a row. The skill of the weaver mostly lies in maintaining the right tension across the weave while it is stretched horizontally, particularly with a wide dhurrie. Warp cotton threads parallel to the ground are stretched across a rectangular structure made of bamboo or other local timber, an almost archaic structure. The weaving is done by throwing the weft thread across the entire width of the stretched warp. No heddles are required to create the shed (the space between sets of warp threads) for a weft-faced plain tabby weave, slitweave, dovetailing or interlocking (all three techniques are used where a change in the colour occurs). The weaver simply lifts alternate warps by hand and throws the weft, usually a stick shuttle with coloured cotton, underneath. The vertical loom is on a much smaller scale, with the weaver sitting in front of his loom on a low stool or on the floor (47). The pit-loom (48), which is also small, seems to have been typically Indian, and is still widely used in Uttar Pradesh in centres of cottage industry, such as Sitapur, and in several jails all over India, such as Yeravda Jail in Poona (Pune). A pit is dug in the earth and the loom fits into it, while the weaver sits on the edge of the pit. It is known as a *karga* pit-loom, and was developed by a cloth weaver in Patna in the late nineteenth century – Patna was then the largest weaving centre in Bengal. Because it was small it was one reason for the increase in the number of families weaving at home, while also helping to halve the number of weavers needed to produce a dhurrie.[49]

The comb (51) with its metal teeth (*panja*) is used to tighten the completed weft line by pressing it firmly down. A curved knife is used for trimming. A *talim* (numbered card) or cartoon is occasionally employed as an aid for copying complex patterns (38).

49
Weavers working on horizontal looms, Jodhpur Central Jail, Rajasthan.

50

Right Detail of red, indigo and white prayer dhurrie with weft-float decoration. Coloured wefts ornament the front face of the weave, floating at the back of the textile when not needed.

51

Below Tools of the trade, combs with metal teeth used by weavers to push down the wefts.

Weaves

Flatweaving is the process of interlacing a warp thread with a weft thread. It is the simplest and fastest way of producing a woven textile. Colours and patterns are introduced once the basic weaving knowledge is acquired. Flatweaving, however, unlike carpet-knotting, limits the possibilities for creating intricate patterns, and this has had a great influence on the design of a rug or dhurrie. The basic weaves, and the more complicated – dovetailing, slitweave, eccentric wefting – are illustrated in the drawings that decorate the endpapers, and are explained in the Glossary.

Selvedges are the side finishes of the dhurrie (see endpaper diagrams). The strength of the selvedges is important as dhurries have to withstand strong wear and tear. Tassels or fringes prevent the dhurrie from fraying. The most common technique is the warp loop fringe, basically the twisting of the warp threads together when the end beam of the loom is removed from the warps and the loops are cut. With the plaited fringe, warp threads are plaited into bands. The net fringe is favoured in village production, and here the warps are knotted together into groups, then subdivided and knotted again (see endpaper diagrams).

Although it is thought of as a basic floor-covering, the dhurrie requires many skills; spinners, dyers, weavers and above all a sense of artistry to produce a pleasing and harmonious tapestry.

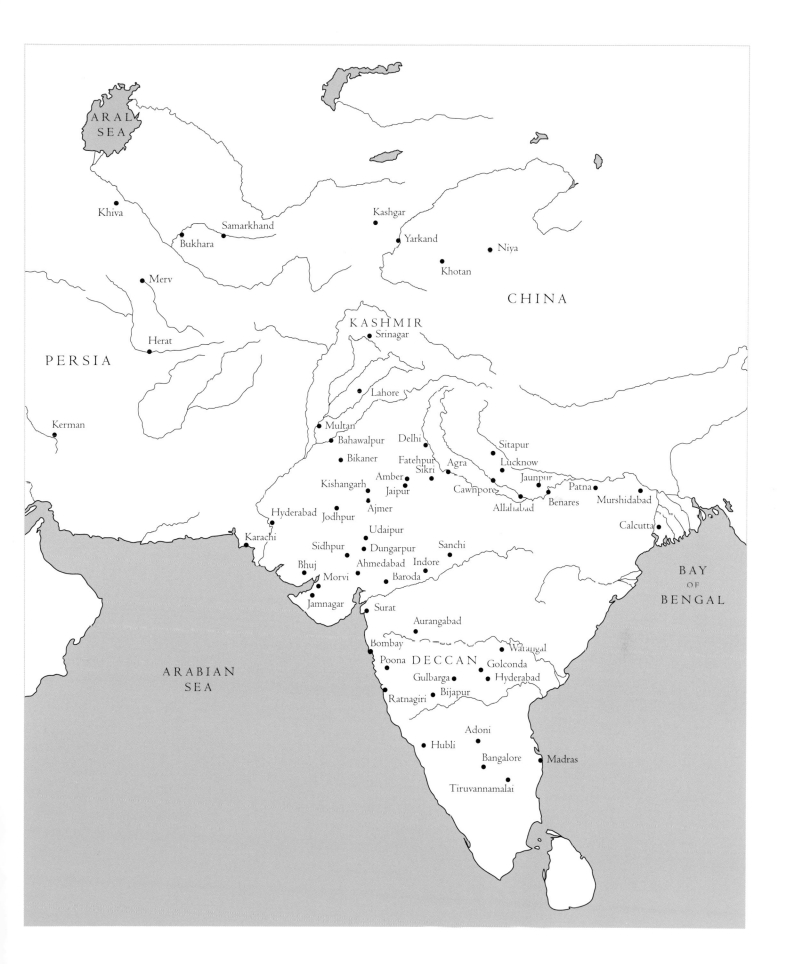

Map of the Indian subcontinent in the 19th century

1 Striped Dhurries

In India people still think of the dhurrie solely in terms of the standard striped floor-covering, with two or three colour combinations — blue and white, or terracotta, blue and white. These were frequently illustrated in Indian miniatures and paintings, and are among the most popular floor-coverings today.

The origin and the popularity of the striped dhurrie are closely related. Stripes are normally the first attempt by an inexperienced weaver to expand his skill through introducing another colour, combining different coloured yarns in alternating bands. The stripes in dhurries have also developed from the stripes in woven reed mats, and from what seems to be a specific Hindu tradition where *sadhus*, or ascetics, are shown seated on tiger skins.[1] In Ajanta, in Cave 1, the dancers are shown sitting on a striped floor-covering, very probably a dhurrie (15), and there are many miniatures from the seventeenth century onwards showing large striped floor-coverings in use for ceremonies and gatherings (53). Furthermore, abstract patterns, whether striped or geometric, appeal both to the Hindu and Muslim communities, and constitute the fundamental vocabulary of dhurrie designs.

Striped dhurries were also favoured by the British, and most of the dhurries brought back to Europe at the end of British rule in India in 1947 were striped or geometric flatweaves. Even in mass-produced dhurries, the permutations of design and the imaginative use of colour still manage to surprise and delight the most experienced dhurrie collector.

Many of these dhurries have a dual purpose. They replace carpets in spring and autumn when the marble or tile floors are still too cool to be left bare, and they also serve as outdoor floor-coverings during religious festivals and large gatherings or

52

Interior, Bagru House, Jaipur, with a late 19th-century large indigo and white dhurrie. T. C. Goel/Samurai Collection.

53

Tansi Thakur Bag Singh and his court, attributed to S. Ram
Narayan, Rajasthan, 1880, opaque watercolour on paper,
Collection of Prince and Princess Sadruddin Aga Khan.

encampments. Striped dhurries are also used as everyday bedding, work surfaces or outdoor seating. Outdoor *durbars*, or audiences, and festivals provide occasions all over India for the use of these striped dhurries — large or small according to the importance of the event. The use of striped dhurries for large Hindu festivals and other ceremonies, therefore, draws on a long-standing tradition in the Hindu way of life. During Holi, the spring festival of colour when people throw paints and pigments at each other (5), plain striped dhurries are used, and coloured stains can often be seen on the large blue and white expanse of the dhurries of Gujarat and Rajasthan.

In view of this, Sir George Birdwood's opinion that the striped dhurrie is mainly a Hindu textile is understandable, but the widespread use of blue and white striped dhurries among the Muslim population of India relates to the use of similar rugs in Persia (Iran), where there was a long tradition of blue and white floor-coverings — blue and white *ikat* (resist-dyed cotton) floor-coverings or tiles for dignitaries to stand on, and blue and white *zilu*, or rugs, in the mosques, particularly at the shrine of Ni'matullah in Mahan outside Kerman (54). The geometric field of this *zilu* is surrounded by a calligraphic border citing the terms of the patron's donation to the shrine.[2] *Zilus* are a form of flatweave, produced on a draw loom, and may have had a certain influence on Indian dhurrie design — the intricate geometric

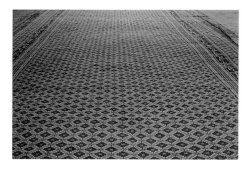

54

Blue and white *zilu* with calligraphic border, *c.* 1850, shrine of Ni'matullah, Mahan, Iran. Photo courtesy Professor Michael Rogers.

55

Terracotta, blue and white striped dhurrie with a feathered diamond-patterned border, Rajasthan, probably Ajmer, *c.* 1880. 3.28 x 10.45m, 10ft 9in x 13ft 6in. T. C. Goel/Samurai Collection.

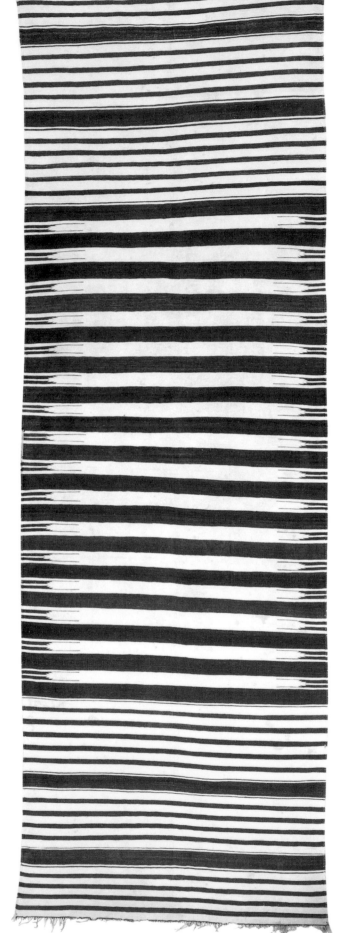

pattern and the two colours are a distinctive feature also found in India. This fascination of blue and white for people who have mastered the art of dyeing probably arose mainly from the earlier influence of blue and white Chinese porcelain, and also perhaps from the predominance of the blue and white tiles in the mosques of Iran and areas of Persian influence in the Punjab, such as Multan, and the village of Hala which produced the favourite blue and white tiles of India.[3]

The preference for blue and white also reflects the supreme importance of water and its cooling effect, often represented in Indian miniatures. Water tanks and ornamental pools are an essential feature of many temples, mosques, shrines and palaces, especially in the hot dry state of Rajasthan. In a miniature painted in Rajasthan, Krishna and Radha are shown in a pool surrounded by water-jets lined up like the flower pots (56). The white water-jets on the blue ground of the pool could very well have been transformed into the designs of the blue and white dhurries so favoured in Rajasthan.

Large Striped

Religious ceremonies were not the only occasion when large striped dhurries were used, for they were greatly favoured in royal households. Most private apartments in palaces and large houses used the striped dhurrie as underlay for more important carpets in winter (74) or printed cloth in summer in the reception rooms. They used them as floor covers in the private rooms, as shown by the sample for the private ladies' apartment in the Nizam of

56

Opposite left Radha and Krishna in a boat, Udaipur or Bikaner School, miniature, *c.* 1860. The Nasser D. Khalili Collection of Islamic Art.

57

Opposite right Blue and white handspun cotton veranda dhurrie, Shekhawati district, Rajasthan, *c.* 1880. 1.96 x 4.26m, 6ft 5in x 14ft. T. C. Goel/Samurai Collection.

58

Left A section of a red and dark blue veranda dhurrie with punch daggers and 'stepped ending' stripe motifs, reputed to have come from the Nizam of Hyderabad's household, Deccan, *c.* 1880, 2.06 x 5.1m, 6ft 9in x 16ft 9in. T. C. Goel/Samurai Collection.

59

Below Section of a large dhurrie with 'stepped ending' stripes, reputed to have come from the Nizam of Hyderabad's household, Deccan, 19th century. 4.88 x 61m, 16 x 20ft. T. C. Goel/Samurai Collection.

60

London interior with a large blue and white dhurrie, Rajasthan, probably Ajmer, c. 1880. Private collection.

Hyderabad's household (21). The large standard striped dhurries were produced in the nineteenth century in great numbers mainly in commercial mills and jail workshops. Most palace *farrashkhanas*, or storerooms,contained large striped dhurries, and in some of the palace storerooms that I visited – in Jodhpur Fort Palace, for instance – I saw geometric and striped dhurries that were stamped MEHRANGAR FORT rolled up and stored for various functions and ceremonies.

An outstanding striped dhurrie (42) is unique in that it was destined for royalty. The indigo and white stripes are interspersed by yellow and pink *mahi* or fish motifs, elongated feathered white, pink and yellow diamonds and feathered pink silk-thread and silver diamonds, with silver-gilt inner motifs. This subtle glittering effect indicates the importance of the commission as well as the fineness of execution. It probably served as an outside floor covering for a *durbar*, as we can see from the wallpainting of the *durbar* scene in the Dungarpur Juna Mahal in Rajasthan (43). It has been suggested that this dhurrie was part of a dowry, but its large size indicates otherwise. It is very interesting how even a common design is transformed into an exquisitely woven piece when the commission is royal.

This tradition of using large dhurries for special occasions was followed by the affluent classes, as seen in an early nineteenth-century miniature from 'The Fraser Album' (61). It depicts a group of musicians under an awning, performing for a marriage or the birth of a son.[4]

The Deccan, particularly Hyderabad, is known for the distinctive design and colour of its striped dhurries, as seen in the dhurrie in pink and a natural colour with 'stepped endings' to the stripe (59).

Storyteller, dancer and musicians, from 'The Fraser Album', Delhi, c. 1810–20. Collection of Prince and Princess Sadruddin Aga Khan.

62

Above Damselle, Awadh School, 19th century.
Lucknow Museum, Uttar Pradesh.

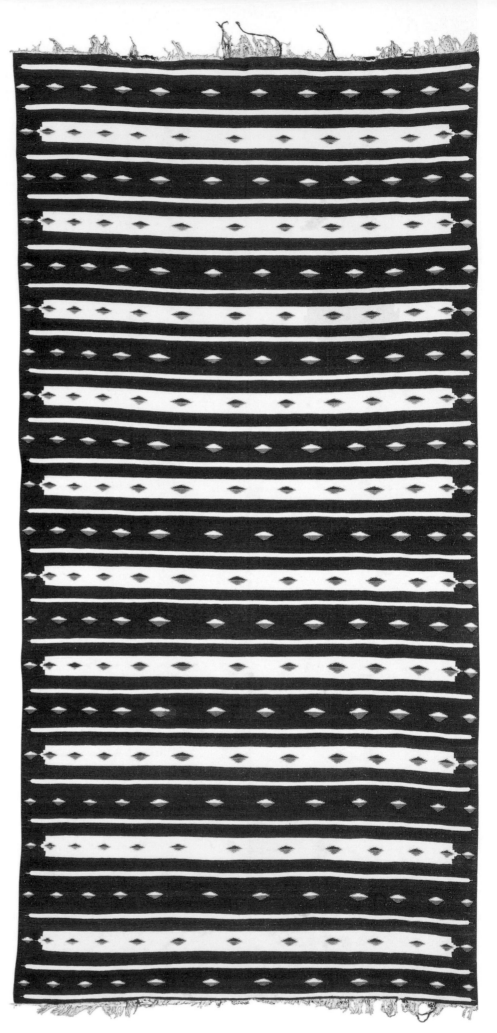

63

Right Indigo, terracotta and white 'double minaret'
striped dhurrie with feathered diamonds, in the Ajmer
style, Rajasthan, *c.* 1880. 1.14 x 2.06m, 3ft 9in x 6ft 9in.
T. C. Goel/Samurai Collection.

64

Opposite above Section of indigo, pale blue, terracotta
and white striped dhurrie with feathered diamonds,
Rajasthan, *c.* 1880. 3.66 x 4.88m, 12 x 16ft.
T. C. Goel/Samurai Collection.

65

Opposite below Section of indigo, pale blue and white
striped dhurrie with stylized *mahi*, terracotta border
with indigo and white feathered diamonds, Rajasthan,
probably Bikaner, *c.* 1880. 3.05 x 4.27m, 10 x 14ft.
T. C. Goel/Samurai Collection.

66

Above Blue and white village striped dhurrie with *mahi* motif, Rajasthan, *c.* 1880. 1.07 x 1.83m, 3ft 6in x 6ft. T. C. Goel/Samurai Collection.

67

Right Blue and white village striped dhurrie with a terracotta and white feathered diamond and *tùbà* tree motif, Rajasthan or Gujarat, *c.* 1880. 1.22 x 1.98m, 4ft x 6ft 6in. T. C. Goel/Samurai Collection.

Small Striped

The small striped dhurries are the most common, and among the most appealing of all the dhurries. Stripes seem to work extremely well as a pattern on such a small scale, and the inventiveness of the Indian weavers, particularly the village women, has produced some of the most effective and dazzling designs. They seem to be primarily part of the bedding of humble folk when they are used on a *charpai*, a wooden and rope bed, as insulation underneath thicker bedding for comfort and coolness (69). The variety of stripes and the number of different combinations is astonishing, and one marvels at all the different permutations.

Among the most arresting are those in indigo and white when used to cover a whole courtyard on a cool evening after a warm day in Rajasthan, as illustrated opposite the titlepage of this book. The colour and pattern recall water and contribute to the cooling effect against the hot sandstone. These dhurries are normally woven by women in the villages of India on a small standard loom and therefore are of a standard size. A certain delicacy is noticeable in the design and execution, and they are generally loosely woven with homespun cotton, having a totally different feel from dhurries woven in jail or commercial workshops, which were intended for the local market. The samples found in the jails testify to this lucrative business. The jail dhurries are normally tightly woven with machine-spun cotton, and lack much of the originality and lustre of the village productions.

Blue and white are the favourite colours in the north of India, particularly in Rajasthan, Gujarat and Uttar Pradesh. They often include a fish or tree motif alluding to their cooling property in

68

Above Blue and white village striped dhurrie with a terracotta and white Tree of Life and feathered diamond motif, Rajasthan or Gujarat, *c.* 1880. 1.14 x 19.05m, 3ft 9in x 6ft 3in. T. C. Goel/Samurai Collection.

69

Right Jami Masjid, Ahmedabad, a *charpai* with a *saf* used as a bed dhurrie.

the rather harsh, drought-prone area of northern India. It is a perfect example of how elements of classical Indian carpet design have been absorbed into the local folklore and the traditional vocabulary of local weaving.

The use of blue and white also has a mystical connotation, a reference to Paradise, more fully discussed in the chapter on prayer dhurries (Chapter 6) – the colours are a reflection in this world of 'Gardens of Eden underneath which rivers flow' (Qur'an, sura 98: 8), water courses flowing in gardens in which trees, fish and flowers abound. The tree, often referred to as the cypress tree because of its shape, is in fact a reference to the *tùbà* tree, 'the wonderful tree in Paradise, more slender and elegant than the cypress'.[5] The great nineteenth-century poet Ghalib goes further in describing his beloved: 'she resembles the shadow of the *tùbà* tree and the river of honey'.[6] Fish, elongated as if moving upstream, are also frequently depicted in these striped dhurries. Some include two-coloured, stepped or feathered diamonds in the decoration, a reference to the silver decoration or shells on some of the other textiles the women produce, and this gives them a jewel-like effect (*71*).

Rajasthan and Gujarat seem to have favoured this style, with variations in the Punjab and Uttar Pradesh. It seems that the design has emerged from Ajmer, a district in Rajasthan, with the emphasis on rhythm created by the contrast between the stripes of the central area and the accentuated *patti* (*71*). Ajmer is one of the most important Chishti shrines in India. The Chishti Sufi order uses music as part of its devotional ritual – the stripes create rhythm and cadence. The devotional and ritualistic aspect noticeable in the prayer dhurries has certainly influenced the local village dhurries with their references to water courses, fish and *tùbà* trees, and also explains why so many have a minaret-type indentation with a standard at each end of the stripes. These dhurries are always referred to as prayer rugs, which they are not – they simply borrow a devotional motif for a secular concept. Stepped diamonds in one or two shades, or the Tree of Life are the only other decorative elements used. On the whole, the reliance of the weaver on the abstract rhythmical blue and white stripe is sufficient to create a masterpiece of simplicity and harmony.

70

Top Section of a striped dhurrie, Uttar Pradesh, *c.* 1880. 2.45 x 1.2m, 8ft ½in x 3ft 11in. AEDTA Collection.

71

Above Striped dhurrie with a constellation of feathered diamonds and smaller motifs, Gujarat, *c.* 1880. 1.22 x 1.93m, 4ft x 6ft 4in. T. C. Goel/Samurai Collection.

72

Opposite above Section of a striped dhurrie with elongated *mahi* motif, Kutch, Gujarat, *c.* 1880. 1.22 x 2.13m, 4 x 7ft. T. C. Goel/Samurai Collection.

73

Opposite below Multi-coloured striped dhurrie with *mahi* motif, Kutch, Gujarat, early 19th century. 1.22 x 2.13m, 4 x 7ft. T. C. Goel/Samurai Collection.

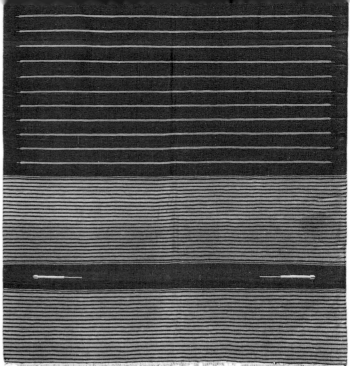

Several versions of the small striped dhurrie exist. Bhuj in Kutch (Kacch) in Gujarat and Bikaner in Rajasthan produced a very soft version of the striped dhurrie which included 'cypress or fish' motifs in indigo, pale blue, sand and white . The example formerly held by the AEDTA collection in Paris (Association de l'Etude et Documentation de Textiles Anciens) is a late nineteenth century village production (70), and has a typical Kutch feature, a weft float brocade technique often used in this region where neighbouring Baluchi tribal weaving had a great influence. The natural dyes have faded, enhancing the handspun cotton texture of the dhurrie. The prevailing sand colour is a great favourite in the Kutch and Bikaner regions because of their proximity to the desert and the influence of artefacts made from goat and camelhair.

Gujarat, a region where madder plants grow, seems to have experimented more with the use of terracotta, while Rajasthan favoured the more traditional indigo and white stripe. A Gujarati striped dhurrie in indigo, pink and terracotta, and with an elongated pink and white *mahi* motif (72) is made of machine spun and tightly woven cotton, obviously a jail production as it lacks the originality of village dhurries. Jails also produced sophisticated striped dhurries such as the one featured here, also from Gujarat, (73) with *mahi* motif, and an unusual combination of colours – indigo, white, terracotta, aquamarine, mauve and burnt orange – indicating the private nature of the commission.

South India also had its own striped dhurrie production. It particularly favoured 'hot' colour combinations, such as red and blue with yellow thin striped highlights, with the occasional inclusion of of silk thread. It was influenced by its famous traditional silk-weaving industry and sari production. It also produced the standard indigo and white striped dhurries as documented by Forbes-Watson in his *Textile Manufactures of the People of India and their Costumes*, but did not include any ornamentations such as trees, fish or stepped diamonds.

As individual bedding or prayer mats, communal floor coverings for religious festivals or multi-niche prayer rugs, the striped dhurrie was adopted and widely used by both Hindu and Muslim communities. It naturally replaced the humble reed mat in both religious and secular contexts.

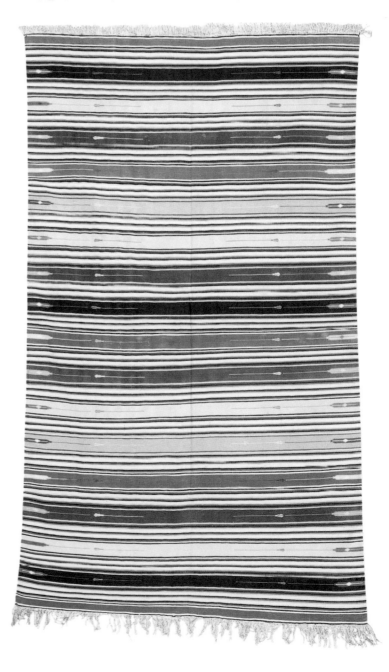

2 *Pictorial Dhurries*

There is an interesting parallel between the patterns that can be seen on the great canvas of the natural world and the patterns illustrated in this group of carpets and dhurries. The imagery, whether dramatic, graphic or lyrical, is always concerned with close human observation of the natural world and the natural order. Nature is a central theme in Indian art. The universe in its multiplicity of life and form is represented by myths and symbols. This concern with the observation of nature was picked up by the Mughals when they conquered India. Babur himself commissioned the first scientific studies of the flora and fauna of his new country, which he discussed in his memoirs. This interest in nature, combined with early Persian influences, form the backdrop of this small and select group of dhurries with spectacular pictorial designs, and that date from the late nineteenth and early twentieth centuries.

These dhurries suggest a certain knowledge of earlier Indian carpet design, which was in its turn influenced by the sixteenth- and early seventeenth-century Persian carpets imported into India. During the period 1500–1700 there was close Indo-Persian cultural intercourse – the Mughals and the Safavid dynasties shared a common heritage, a common language (Persian) and a common religion (Islam). Exchanges between the two empires led to the distinctive carpet designs, miniature paintings and other art forms of this period.

The great epics and legends that permeated the life of the imperial Mughal court were transmitted orally and visually, not only in the many princely courts, but also to a wider public, right up to the twentieth century, through the popular scroll paintings (*pata*) executed by skilled craftsmen.[1] Myths and legends have always been transmitted orally in the East, and the storyteller/painter or bard plays an important role as the keeper of this wisdom. He recites his

74

Interior of Kanota Palace, Kanota, Rajasthan, with Peacock dhurrie, *c.* 1880, on striped dhurrie underlay. T. C. Goel/Samurai Collection.

passages while pointing out in sequence the painted scenes representing the events (75). This strong tradition is the fundamental vehicle for the transmission of ornamentation.

The weaver or cartoon designer operating in jail or commercial workshops was aware of local folklore, and had a strong knowledge of the traditional representation of these popular themes. The interpretation of a theme might be faithful or a variation on it, according to the skill of the weaver, the nature of the commission and a certain freedom of interpretation enjoyed by the designer. This very special group of dhurries, with their elaborate compositions, were all made as private commissions for rich or princely patrons. Although produced in the local jail workshops, these dhurries were of a very superior quality in both materials and workmanship compared with the standard designs produced at that time for a general market.

Noah's Ark

Among the most enchanting of the pictorial dhurries are those representing animals. There are only five versions and five variations in this group. Nineteenth-century British cultural expansion and missionary activity is reflected in their name – they are invariably called after the dhurrie, made around 1915 in Ahmedabad's

76

Detail of Noah's Ark dhurrie in Sabarmati Central Jail,
Ahmedabad, inscribed 'A.C.P. Sample 1915' (ACP stands
for Ahmedabad Central Prison).

77

Left Noah's Ark dhurrie, Ahmedabad, Gujarat, *c.* 1920. 3.05 x 3.13m, 10ft x 10ft 3ins. Photo courtesy Sotheby's.

78

Below Forest landscape with river, opaque watercolour on paper from a manuscript of the *Mahabharata*, dated 1670, south India (Karnataka), probably Seringapatam. Courtesy Jagdish and Kamla Mittal Museum of Indian Art, Hyderabad.

Sabarmati Central Jail (*76 & 35*), which is known as the Noah's Ark dhurrie for obvious reasons – a whole array of animals is shown in procession around the central Ark.[2] But these dhurries also belong to a long line of representations typical of India's cultural heritage combining Hindu, Muslim and Christian beliefs.[3]

That these dhurries also have their origins in early Hindu and Muslim manuscripts can be seen from a miniature (*78*) in a manuscript dated 1670 of the ancient Hindu epic the *Mahabharata* (The Book of Wars), whose main theme is the struggle between the Kaurava and the Pandava families. Jagdish Mittal in *India: Art and Culture, 1300–1900*, writes that this illustration 'could be from the *Aranyaka Parva* (Forest Chapter), which narrates the life of the Pandavas during their exile. The grove of flowering trees beside a river alive with fish and a crocodile could be one of the three forests the Pandavas stayed in…. Pure landscapes like this are rare in Indian art, where nearly every painting has a figural subject.' The composition is divided into three clearly delineated registers, or sections: animals, fish and text. The ordering of the animals and

79
Jackal and fish, detail of a page from *Aja'ib al-Makhluqat*
(Wonders of Creation), Deccan, 16th century.
Private collection.

the trees in the forest, and the circular movement of the fish in the
river, as if in a procession around the crocodile, echo the lines of
the Sanskrit text in the margins. This same two-dimensional
display is clearly found in the composition of the animal dhurries.
In the Noah's Ark dhurrie (77) the inner and outer borders are
decorated with marching animals – peacocks and other exotic creatures – and frame the main field with its own marching animal
procession. Each register is strongly delineated, and represents in
succession the sky, the earth, and the rivers and seas. The influence
of such miniatures on the design of the animal dhurries is further
strengthened by the fact that they are both narratives and are therefore using the same organization of space where the ordering of
the words is mirrored by the juxtaposition of the animals. In view
of the sophistication of the dhurrie design, the weavers must ini-
tially have worked from a cartoon drawn by an artist who was
aware of the Indian tradition in the representation of animals.

The *Mahabharata* is not the only influence on the pictorial
animal dhurries. Al-Qazwini's famous work in Arabic *Aja'ib
al-Makhluqat* (Wonders of Creation), of which there are many illustrated versions, was another source of inspiration (79). It was
widely available in India, particularly in the Deccan, a state that
enjoyed a privileged relationship with the Arab world and was a
great centre of Arab learning in the sixteenth century.[4] Several
copies of al Qazwini's thirteenth-century cosmological treatise
were produced in the Deccan in the sixteenth century, and it was
extremely popular. The representation of the animals in the
manuscript is paralleled in the organization and depiction of the
animals in the dhurries, as is a certain folk quality and the fascination for the theme of the Creation.

It is interesting to trace other artistic influences, in early carvings of animals, for example. There is a thirteenth-century
architectural complex at Dabhoi, 29 kilometres (18 miles) from
Baroda (Vadodara), in the state of Maharashtra where only four
gates and a temple survive. In the carvings on the exterior walls the
half-lotus motif, the row of *hamsa*, or geese (80), and the row of
elephants and soldiers correspond to the rows of peacocks and
of alternating exotic creatures found in the inner and outer border
of the Ark dhurries.

80

Sandstone frieze carved in relief of *hamsa*, or geese, 13th century, Dabhoi, Maharashtra.

Animal deities, such as Humayun the monkey god and the elephant-headed Ganesh, and sacred animals, such as the peacock, Nandi the bull and Garuda the mythical bird, play an important part in the Hindu pantheon. It is therefore not surprising that they form the basis of the Indian visual decorative vocabulary, as we have seen in the scrolls.

In a late nineteenth-century embroidery from eastern India (81) there is a rather different treatment of the representation of animals, unrestricted by the rigid organization of space of the Ark dhurries. The animals are placed haphazardly as if in a dance or ritual, and this free composition suggests a certain 'primitive' quality.

Finally, it is clear that the classical carpet, which again has a close relationship with manuscript illumination, has also influenced these animal dhurries. There is a group of early pictorial Indian carpets of the late sixteenth to the early seventeenth

81

Kantha, or embroidery, late 19th century, western Bengal, Courtesy Jagdish and Kamla Mittal Museum of Indian Art, Hyderabad.

82

Carpet with pictorial design, Lahore. *c.* 1590–1600.
2.43 x 1.54m, 7ft 11½in x 5ft ½in. Museum of Fine Arts,
Boston.

83

Fragment of a carpet with fantastic animals, probably
Fatehpur Sikri, *c.* 1580–85. 1.52 x 1.13m, 5ft x 3ft 8½in.
The Textile Museum, Washington, DC.

centuries depicting fantastic animals. The only example surviving complete is now in the Museum of Fine Arts in Boston, Massachusetts (82). This carpet is divided into three clear registers with a central vertical scroll of flowers and foliage connecting the three scenes – a palace scene above, a hunting scene in the middle and a scene with fantastic animals in the lower register. This sophisticated weaving of the narrative of the main field within a border of alternating fantastic birds and blossoms containing grotesques and imaginary animals is a very good example of the traditional representation of animals in Indian carpets. In 1996 Steven Cohen published an essay on other extraordinary carpets with fantastic animal motifs of which only fragments are known (83).[5] A perhaps more immediate carpet source for the Ark dhurries is the early seventeenth-century 'garden' carpet (84) that used to belong to the Maharajas of Jaipur and is now in the Jaipur Museum.[6] Essential features of the garden are the water basins and canals. An array of marine creatures and exotic animals swim in formation along the waterways and in a circular motion around the pavilion in the central basin. The pavilion corresponds to the Ark in the animal dhurries.

Whatever the sources of the iconography, one should not underestimate the artistic imagination and skill of the weaver. Other animal dhurries are a simplified version of the Ark composition, as in the two illustrated overleaf (85 & 87), and a tribute to the creativity of the weaver who, after all, chose the patterns and colours. He also introduced motifs that were of interest

84
Garden carpet (detail), the central basin with
a pavilion, marine creatures and exotic animals, Kerman
(Persia), early 17th century. Jaipur Museum, Jaipur.

to him, just as a later variation of the Ark dhurries included
soldiers and aeroplanes in the composition, introducing new
and topical themes.[7]

A slightly different pictorial dhurrie, which also belongs to
this specially commissioned group, has an enchanting marine and
landscape theme (86). The foreground with a selection of rowing
boats with sailors, dhows, men-of war and steamers is set against a
background of hills, bungalows, trees and a fortified castle with
seagulls and crescent moon in the blue sky.

The inspiration is clearly from two different pictures probably
seen by the designer and in the possession of the individual who
commissioned the dhurrie. The Maharajas of India were great collectors of nineteenth-century British paintings and regularly
purchased pictures from the London Royal Academy Exhibitions.
There were numerous English and Scottish paintings of ships or
rugged landscapes in private collections in India. The source
of this picture must be two paintings, one a seascape and the
other a Scottish landscape. According to the dhurrie's owner,
Joss Graham, it comes from Ahmedabad. It was originally pre-
sented as a gift to the family from the Nawab of Radhanpur,
Radhanpur State, Gujarat, at the turn of the nineteenth and
twentieth centuries, and was commissioned from a jail, most
probably Sabarmati Jail in Ahmedabad which seems to have
favoured this genre of pictorial dhurries at that time.

The exuberance that emanates from this group of pictorial
dhurries is in keeping with the narrative interest of the
designer/weaver in depicting the thrill of Creation and the
abundance of the universe.

85

Pictorial dhurrie with animals, inscribed U.C.K.,
probably a village production, northern India, *c.* 1920.
10.2 x 17.8cm, 4 x 7in. T. C. Goel/Samurai Collection.

86
Pictorial dhurrie with castle and ships, Gujarat, c. 1920.
0.99 x 1.83m, 3ft 3in x 6ft. Courtesy Joss Graham.

87
Pictorial dhurrie with crocodile and leopards,
Gujarat, c. 1900. 1.14 x 1.83 m, 3ft 9in x 6ft. T. C. Goel/
Samurai Collection.

Peacock

Two dhurries, the most outstanding of this pictorial group, depict birds and trees in a landscape, expressions of a favourite Indian folk myth of birds in a jungle. They were certainly royal commissions – one of the only two known examples on a large scale is displayed in Ramnagar Fort, just outside Benares (Varanasi) as part of the collection in the Maharaja of Benares' Vidyamarti Museum. The other is illustrated here (88). These intriguing and important dhurries can be associated with the late sixteenth-century Mughal pictorial carpet in the Österreichisches Museum in Vienna (89). The composition of birds and trees on a red ground in the carpet is the same as that in the dhurries; and the division into three horizontal registers is also there, supplemented in the dhurries, owing to their size, by three vertical registers. Both fields are framed by a repeat pattern border – classical palmette and foliage border in the carpet and peacocks in the dhurries.

88

Peacock dhurrie, Ratnagiri, *c.* 1880. 4.72 x 5.33m, 15ft 6in x 17ft 6in. T. C. Goel/Samurai Collection.

89

Left Carpet with pictorial design, Lahore, *c.* 1590–1600, 2.35 x 1.56m, 7ft 8½in x 5ft 1½in, Österreichisches Museum für Angewandte Kunst, Vienna.

90

Below Nal Daman, dated 1698, Hyderabad, Deccan. Prince of Wales Museum, Bombay (Mumbai).

91

Above Peacock in a Rainstorm, northern Deccan, late 16th century. Private collection.

The composition in the Vienna carpet seems to be a simplified form of that in a miniature in a Deccani Urdu manuscript dated 1698,[8] now in the Prince of Wales Museum, Bombay (Mumbai). The manuscript is the *Nal Daman*, a version of the romance of Nala and Damayanti from the *Mahabharata* (90). The composition of the miniature is clearly divided into an ascending diagonal three-tier register to suggest a foreground, a middle ground and a background, leading the viewer into the picture. In the carpet the main field is divided horizontally into three registers, each depicting trees with birds, within a border of classical palmette and foliage, animals and grotesques. In the dhurrie (88), the central field is divided into five vertical registers, each consisting of a tree with peacocks and fowls within a peacock and foliage border.

The theme was treated poetically in a late sixteenth-century northern Deccani painting from the *Ragamala*, *Peacock in a Rainstorm* (91), where at the time of mating the male peacock 'flies from tree to tree shrieking his mating cry, startling tiny birds roosting in

92

Detail of Peacock dhurrie *101*, with peahen
and elongated leaves, *c.* 1880. T. C. Goel/Samurai
Collection.

delicate new foliage'.[9] These Peacock dhurries, according to tradition, were produced in Ratnagiri Jail which at the time was part of
the northern Deccan and so may have been influenced by this
painting style. The choice of a red ground is also relevant; the
expression of mood through colour is a long established tradition
in India where the word *raga* refers not only to mood but also to
colour in particular dyes. According to P. Jayakar, 'colours were
surcharged with nuances of mood and poetic association. Red was
the colour evoked between lovers: a local Hindi couplet enumer-
ates three tones of red, to evoke the three states of love; of these,
manjitha, madder was the fastest, for like the dye, it could never be
washed away.'[10] Most certainly a reference to the intensity of
passion of love is represented in the Peacock dhurries.

Stylistically the two large Peacock dhurries are very similar to
the designs and techniques found in Chinese silk panels of the
northern Song dynasty known as *kesi* (*93*). In both the dhurries and
kesi is found a horizontal narrative rhythm, and stylized flora and
fauna, with an emphasis on elongated branches and leaves, interspersed with animals and birds. Making a connection between the
two flatweaves is irresistible. Both share the same technique:
tapestry or weft face plain tabby weave. More recently the *kesi* have
been attributed to western China, the territory of the Uighurs,
also known to have had a tapestry-weaving tradition.[11] *Kesi* weaves
were originally used as covers for books and ceremonial scrolls and
could have reached India as part of religious exchanges between
Buddhist monasteries from China via Central Asia.

93

Detail of silk *kesi* panel, China, 10th–12th century.
52 x 34.5cm, 1ft 8½in x 1ft 1½in. Courtesy Spink
& Son Ltd.

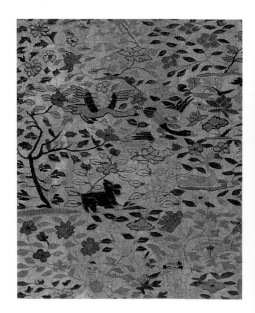

The theme of 'birds in a jungle' was very popular in India, and it was also used for Indian textile exports, as a painted eighteenth-century *palampore*, or bedcover, demonstrates (95). The field is divided into three registers: a vase and a flowering tree with ducks and birds in the centre, and a bamboo tree on either side. The composition is a faithful interpretation of the subject.

A more recent and interesting interpretation of peacocks in a landscape can be found in a Rajasthani *pechwai*, or painted cloth hanging, dating from the mid-nineteenth century (94). This is a strikingly rhythmical composition, with rows of peacocks facing each other, interspersed with peahens, in a moonlit landscape. The whole composition has been interpreted as either the god and goddess Krishna and Radha, or Krishna's dalliance with the *gopis* (milkmaids).[12] Peacocks and peahens are often associated with Krishna. These associations between certain animals and deities exemplify the idea of partnership between humans and animals in relation to the divine. This preoccupation with the representation of animals as an essential part of understanding the universal can be seen in floor paintings as well as carvings, miniatures and dhurries.

In the smaller versions of the Peacock dhurries overleaf (97 & 98), the treatment of the peacocks and the peahens is not as successful. Their colours and their composition lack the intensity and originality of the *pechwai* painting or the two larger Peacock dhurries.

94
Below left Pechwai, peacocks and peahens, Rajasthan, mid-19th century. 2.31 x 1.8m, 7ft 6¾in x 5ft 11in. Harvard University Art Museums.

95
Below right Chintz *palampore*, two bamboo trees with a central flowering tree, Coromandel Coast, *c.* 1740. 2.29 x 1.82m, 7ft 6in x 5ft 11½in. Courtesy Spink & Son Ltd.

96

Detail of Peacock dhurrie 88 with peacock, peahens
and other fowl among flowering branches and leaves,
c. 1880. T. C. Goel/Samurai Collection.

97

Above Pictorial dhurrie with peacocks, Ratnagiri,
c. 1900. 2.13 x 1.30m, 7ft x 4ft 3in. T. C. Goel/Samurai
Collection.

98

Left Pictorial dhurrie with peacock and peahens,
Ratnagiri, *c.* 1900. 2.13 x 1.30m, 7ft x 4ft 3in. T. C. Goel/
Samurai Collection.

Hunting

In India animals were closely studied and featured in myths and legends. In the great pattern of life, some, like the deer, were considered natural prey, and others, like the tiger, worthy opponents of the hunter. The rulers of India rode into battle on horses; the prowess of the rider and the swiftness of his mount were essential for survival. It is only natural that hunting was seen as a sport, and symbolized the respect that human beings felt for animals.

Hunting scenes are a great favourite in the early carpets and miniature paintings of India, and it is not surprising that they also figure in the dhurrie. In the late nineteenth-century hunting dhurrie illustrated (*100*) the division of the field into three diagonal registers, and the stylized animals and trees, notably the palms, are very similar to the arrangement found in the Morgan carpet at the Metropolitan Museum (*99*). Here again, as in the Noah's Ark and Peacock dhurries, we have a direct reference to sixteenth- and seventeenth-century carpets produced in Lahore, and a composition certainly originating in miniature painting (see *90*). The border is similar to that of the sixteenth-century dhurrie from Lahore, now in the Calico Museum of Textiles in Ahmedabad, and to the borders of illuminated manuscripts with poppies, narcissi and other flowers.

The exuberant hunting dhurrie, *c.* 1910, illustrated as *102*, is a more direct copy of the hunting or animal carpets produced in Lahore between 1620 and 1630 (such as the example in the National Gallery of Art, Washington, DC, Widener Collection). The dark blue indigo field with eight riders chasing deer, rabbits, cheetahs and tigers in a forest is enclosed within a natural border of alternating feathered medallions in pale blue and crimson. The vibrancy of the pale blue, yellow, crimson and browns against a dark blue ground is echoed by the dynamic movements of the riders and animals. The designer must have drawn inspiration from hunting miniatures, as the variety of animals and the different representations of riders and horses demonstrate. The border is also an interpretation of the cartouche borders found in carpets and manuscripts. This is a very expressive dhurrie, and the skill involved is notable. It was probably produced in northern India and is the only example that I know of.

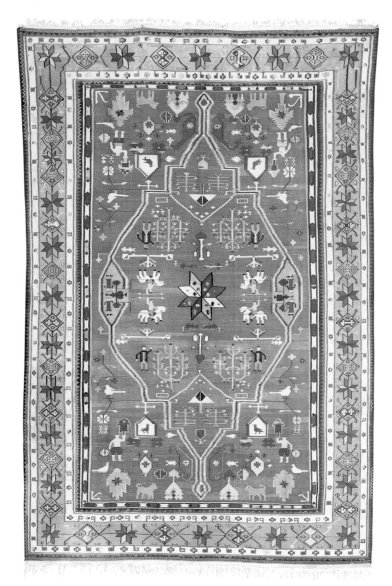

99

Opposite above Section of a carpet with pictorial designs, Lahore, late 16th–early 17th century, 8.33 x 2.9m, 27ft 4in x 9ft 6in. The Metropolitan Museum of Art, New York.

100

Opposite below Pictorial dhurrie with hunter and animals, late 19th century, northern India, 1.22 x 2.13m, 4 x 7ft. Courtesy David Black.

101

Left Pictorial dhurrie with medallion and hunting scenes, *c.* 1910, Rajasthan. 1.63 x 2.67m, 5ft 4in x 8ft 9in. T. C. Goel/Samurai Collection.

102

Below Pictorial dhurrie with hunting scenes, *c.* 1910, northern India. 1.22 x 2.13m, 4 x 7ft. Courtesy Marzbeen P. Jila.

The medallion hunting dhurrie (*101*) of around 1910 has a different composition, and a subject matter more allied to folklore. The central field comprises a large 'feathered' central medallion outlined in white on a blue ground with an eight-pointed flower in the centre defining the invisible line from which the 'mirror' composition emanates. The field is decorated with huntsmen on horses, uniformed men on foot,[13] trees, animals and various decorations, all enclosed within a stylized star-and-diamond border. The overall pale ground and border, with delicate and restrained decoration, lend the dhurrie a jewel-like quality. I know of four such dhurries, all woven with the finest quality cotton and probably all special commissions. This is certainly a bed dhurrie because of its size, the quality of the cotton and the fineness of execution – the 'mirror-image' composition lends itself to this function as the design can read from either end of the bed.

Façade of a *haveli* in Fatehpur, Shekhawati, Rajasthan, with elephants and riders, *c.* 1890.

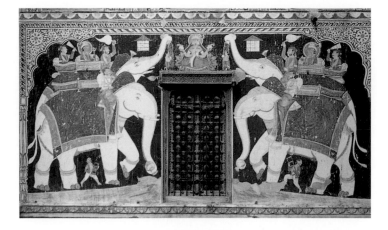

In *The Unappreciated Dhurrie*,[14] Steven Cohen suggests that in view of the fact that similar pieces were widely produced in central jails in Uttar Pradesh it would be fair to assume that this theme is specific to this state. I would tend to agree with him, as the European figures depicted are reminiscent of figures found in Company School paintings (made by Indian artists for British patrons), and, according to Huyler, legendary heroes, peacocks, horses, monkeys, dogs, flowers and foliate forms are a common feature in the visual arts in Uttar Pradesh, often painted on walls and floors.[15] Furthermore, the stylized horse and rider represents the legendary King Pramachandan whose epic story is told to children to inspire heroic virtues.[16] According to its owner, however, the dhurrie illustrated as *101* was especially commissioned from Jaipur Central Jail, Rajasthan, in 1910, and it does share a certain enchanting naive quality found in the mural paintings of the merchant's *havelis*, or mansions, in the nearby Shekhawati district of Rajasthan (*103*). This example highlights the general problem of provenance – it would have been easy to copy dhurries in view of the skills found in the jails in the early twentieth century and of the way patterns travelled from jail to jail with the superintendents.[17] To complicate matters further, this particular dhurrie was a special commission and the client most probably provided the jail with cotton of a superior quality.

It is not surprising that hunting scenes were commissioned by rulers in this long tradition of the representation of the chase. Hunting was a class privilege, and also symbolized the ruler's right over matters of life and death. Only royalty was allowed to hunt lions and tigers. In India it was a rite of passage for any young nobleman or noblewoman.

Left Tree of Life *jali*, Sidi Sayed Mosque (built 1572), Ahmedabad, Gujarat, 19th-century photograph.

Tree of Life and Vase

Although the Tree of Life is a motif common throughout the ancient cultures of the Orient, it has a particular significance in India because of its association with the Hindu worship of trees. After painting the ground in front of their dwelling, the women proceed to paint the ground under an ancient tree nearby, emphasizing its importance in their daily ritual.[18] According to Dr T. S. Maxwell, 'Early Hindu attempts at expressing cult philosophies through complex images were artistically controlled and religiously validated by the holiness of the tree.'[19]

The Tree of Life dhurries are very attractive, and among the most spectacular is a dhurrie in the Crafts Museum in Delhi, dating from around 1900 (*105 & 106*). The main field is divided vertically into three registers with alternating small blue and yellow vases. From each vase issues a mango tree covering the ivory surface of the dhurrie, all within a border of meandering vine and mango branches on an orange ground. Mirror symmetry is an important component of the composition because of its semi-abstract quality, a feature that it shares with *kilims* (the Turkish term for a woollen flatweave), particularly Tribal Anatolian *kilims*. In *kilims*, as in this dhurrie, a motif is woven up to the central invisible axis of

105 & 106

Above and left Details of Tree of Life dhurrie, with mangoes and leaves and a Gujarati inscription, *c.* 1900. 9.1 x 4.45m, 29ft 10in x 14ft 7in (entire). Courtesy Crafts Museum, New Delhi.

the surface then symmetrically mirrored on the other side. This dhurrie was most probably woven in Ahmedabad Central Jail, Gujarat; its size would certainly have required an extra-large loom, and these were to be found mostly in jail workshops. It is inscribed in Gujarati 'Abdul Hussain Daoudji Lakdawala: Sidhpur.' Sidhpur is a town inhabited by the Bohras, a community of wealthy Muslim merchants who built extravagant houses at the turn of the twentieth century and furnished them with dhurries. The direct source of inspiration for this dhurrie is the classical Persian Vase and Tree carpet developed in Lahore in the sixteenth and seventeenth centuries, and a further obvious influence is the pierced stone screen, or *jali,* depicting a tree at the Sidi Sayed Mosque (built in 1572) in Ahmedabad (*104*) and the various tree and flower paintings in the tomb of Jahangir in Lahore.

There is another large Tree of Life and Vase dhurrie of around 1910 (*107*), probably produced in Bikaner Central Jail, Rajasthan, as a sample found in the jail shows (*108*). It has an even more elaborate mirror-image composition. The field is divided horizontally by a central axis representing a stream with fish, then each half is again divided symmetrically, two vases with a Tree of Life branching out facing another pair of vases with trees. The vertical and

107

Above Tree of Life dhurrie, Bikaner, *c.* 1910. 2.74 x 5.15m, 9ft x 17ft. T. C. Goel/Samurai Collection.

108

Left Sample representing Tree of Life with fowl and meandering vine border, Bikaner Central Jail.

horizontal symmetries are again reminiscent of the organization of space found in *kilims*, although the fourfold division of the field is like that of Garden carpets. Both Vase and Garden carpets seem to be direct influences on this dhurrie. The main field is surrounded by two borders, one containing an octagonal flowerhead and meandering vine, and the other a geometric and stylized flowerhead and vine border.

A third example is a magnified version (*109*), probably woven in Bikaner Jail around 1900. It consists of a natural coloured main field with a mirror-image composition of a large stylized flowering plant flanked by two smaller plants based on the Mughal niche and flower style carpets, in particular the large poppy plant carpets (*110*). The design is here greatly simplified,

109

Left Pictorial dhurrie with flowering plant, Bikaner, *c.* 1900. 2 x 1.2m, 6ft 6¾in x 3ft 11in. Courtesy David Black.

110

Above Carpet with niche and flowering plant, northern India, *c.* 1630–40. 1.57 x 1.02cm, 5ft 2in x 3ft 4in. Private collection.

almost graphic, lending the dhurrie a folk quality. The main feature in both carpet and dhurrie is a large plant with five blossoms, in the dhurrie version three yellow blooms at the top and two stylized ones on each side. The *mihrab*, or niche, in the Mughal carpet suggests depth which in the dhurrie is provided by the contrast between the pale central field and the strong colours of the borders. The oversized, large-blossomed plant in a vase within a frame occurs in earlier Indian iconography, as in the Buddhist stone relief of the first century BC from Sanchi, in the state of Madhya Pradesh, where the Vase of Plenty is set between pillars, a raised ground and a lintel.[20] The subject, *purna kalasa*, or Vase of Plenty, has several connotations in India, in particular symbolizing the Devi or Goddess.[21] The varying treatments of this theme across the centuries is typical of the cross-cultural strands in India (*112*).

The final examples, dated 1920–30, show an entirely different version of the Tree of Life and Vase motif. In the 1920s and 1930s

111

Left Pictorial dhurrie with Vase of Plenty, Murshidabad, *c.* 1925. 2.44 x 3.66m, 8 x 12ft. T. C. Goel/Samurai Collection.

112

Above top Sandstone panel with Vase of Plenty, *c.* 1600. Vrindavan, Uttar Pradesh.

113

Above Pictorial dhurrie with flowering plants, Bikaner, *c.* 1910. 1.91 x 1.4m, 6ft 3in x 4ft 7in. Courtesy Sotheby's.

the treatment of this popular theme was adapted to the taste of the time. English motifs and dark 'Victorian' colours were very much in demand.[22] In the dhurrie (*111*) the maroon central field and the Hindu votive oil lamps emulating neoclassical shaped vases and Europeanized arabesques are very Victorian, and, although the double mirror-image still prevails, the choice of flowers and their naturalistic treatment are reminiscent of the nineteenth-century British Arts and Crafts Movement. Even the main borders have European motifs, such as the chain links, and the scrolling leaves and Morning Glory design. Many of these dhurries are reputed to have been favoured and commissioned by members of the Marwari community, Hindu merchants who built large *haveli*s, or mansions, in their place of origin in the Shekhawati district of Rajasthan, but the dhurries are said to have been made in Murshidabad, a great weaving centre in Bengal which supplied most of this community who made its wealth in Calcutta.

There is another larger dhurrie of the same type and date (*114*), with a maroon ground and a large pale blue border. In this the mirror images of the Tree of Life motif, distinctively Indian, meet in a central medallion in the shape of a *bagh*, or garden. Only the maroon field and the stylized heart-shaped flowers on the tree are a vague reminder of Victorian influences. This design was inspired by the popular painted *palampores*, or bedcovers, that were exported in the eighteenth century to England and Holland, and in which the tree emerges from a little mound.

If we compare this dhurrie to the sample from Bikaner Central Jail (*108*), it would seem to be one of those commissioned from that jail for a Shekhawati *haveli*. The weaver must have been trying to emulate the very popular dhurries from Murshidabad, and in many ways it is a much happier combination of colour and design. The large expanse of the pale blue border and the delicacy of the design in the central field give the dhurrie an overall lightness despite the rather overwhelming maroon. The stylized border patterns are also characteristic of Bikaner Central Jail, particularly the geometric scroll and flower borders.

In these dhurries, trees, flowers and foliage wonderfully represent nature. They capture its rhythm, pulse and harmony.

114

Pictorial dhurrie with Tree of Life design, Bikaner, *c.* 1925. 4.57 x 2.74m, 15 x 9ft. T. C. Goel/Samurai Collection.

3 *Floral Dhurries*

Floral designs have always been among the favourite designs for both carpets and flatweaves, in spite of the technical difficulties in rendering these in flatweaves. The whole concept of an endless repeat pattern suggesting Paradise is a notion that appealed to Muslim rulers throughout the ages. Persian influence is again to be found here, and it was further strengthened when the emperor Humayun (1530–56) was given asylum by the Safavid ruler Shah Tahmasp. On Humayun's return to India, he brought with him two of the leading Persian court painters. During the sixteenth and seventeenth centuries, Persian influence on Indian Mughal textiles made it very difficult to distinguish between the two.

The rulers of India particularly favoured this floral theme. Under their patronage, the flora of India was carefully studied and reproduced in several art forms. These were often highly intricate designs, and would most certainly have first appeared as cartoons or drawings in the royal workshop, subsequently adapted to other art forms such as architecture, carpets, miniature borders or metalwork.

The floral schemes were scrolling vine or blossom motifs, either repeated or arranged in a lattice. Indian floral designs with their often oversized flowers and individual interpretation contribute to the dynamic composition of an otherwise traditional motif. Even the choice of colours is typically Indian. This floral style was to be closely associated with the Mughals, as it is often linked to the floral marble inlays of the Taj Mahal. Even the weavers of prayer rugs, which were normally understated, could not resist floral decoration.

115

Puja Room, Bagru House, Jaipur, with a Scrolling Vine and Blossom dhurrie, *c.* 1900. T. C. Goel/Samurai Collection.

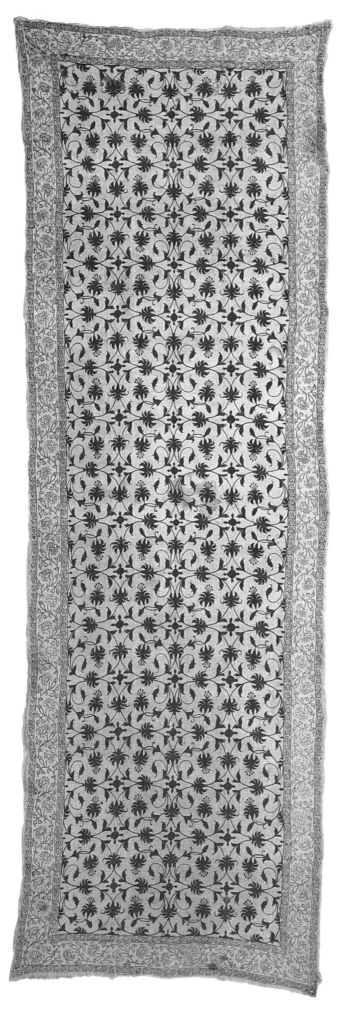

Scrolling Vine and Blossom

The Scrolling Vine and Blossom motif, a design favoured by both Hindus and Muslims, has a contemplative quality. The movement and rhythm suggested by the overall design is reminiscent of cosmic diagrams and cycles. It echoes the divine energy that pulsates in all aspects of the Creation. The Scrolling Vine and Blossom Indian carpets of the early seventeenth century are perhaps the most faithful copies of their Persian counterparts. The overall design is often symmetrical around the central axis and across several other horizontal axes.

With its Scrolling Vine and Blossom design, the so-called Herati-type carpet was one of India's most successful commercial exports, and is often depicted in seventeenth-century Dutch paintings. Bikaner State was renowned for its collection of carpets that came from places ranging from Turkey to Eastern Turkestan, and this collection inspired the designs of the high-quality carpets and dhurries produced in Bikaner Central Jail – these were awarded numerous medals between 1900 and 1937 which are still displayed in the prison. The curves of the Scrolling Vine and Blossom design in a carpet are difficult to reproduce in a flatweave, so the design has to be adapted, simplified and stylized for a dhurrie.

The finest interpretation of the Scrolling Vine and Blossom design in a dhurrie is seen in an early twentieth-century dhurrie (118). The execution and choice of colour compares with nineteenth-century European needlework rugs with their deliberate choice of pale colours and occasional contrasting dark blue

116

Opposite above Mughal silk embroidered and quilted cotton summer carpet with Scrolling Vine and Blossom design, *c.* 1800. 4.10 x 1.35m, 15ft 1½in x 4ft 5in. Courtesy Sotheby's.

117

Opposite below Section of a carpet, eastern Turkestan, with Vine and Blossom design, early 20th century. 3.94 x 2.06m, 12ft 11in x 6ft. Courtesy Christie's.

118

Right Scrolling Vine and Blossom dhurrie, Bikaner, *c.* 1900. 2.67 x 2.13m, 8ft 9in x 7ft. T. C. Goel/Samurai Collection.

119

Scrolling Vine and Blossom sample, Bikaner Central Jail, *c.* 1900.

blossom adding to the dramatic effect of these needlework rug designs. This dhurrie was woven in Bikaner Jail, as a fragment of a similar sample pattern from the jail shows (*119*), and was most definitely a royal commission and part of a dowry. The main composition is a simplified and stylized version of the Scrolling Vine and Blossom design, retaining the repeat element and the vertical mirror-image symmetry of the classical carpet design. The natural central ground is enclosed within three alternating pink and natural borders with a stylized blossom motif. This particular interpretation of the Scrolling Vine and Blossom design also derives from the treatment of the motif in carpets from Eastern Turkestan, Khotan in particular (*117*). The ivory ground, the vertical central axis, the geometric and organic ascent of the vine and blossom, as well as the treatment of the border, are features common to both.

A very successful and delicate combination of colours is similarly used in the sample from Bikaner Central Jail (*119*). The central ground is aquamarine and the borders are in a deep shade of pink and cream, picking up the tonality of the blossoms in the main field. The fine design and execution accord with the tradition and reputation of the Bikaner Jail workshop.

Another version of this classical motif has been adapted to twentieth-century taste. A dhurrie from Benares (Varanasi, Uttar Pradesh) of around 1920 (*120*) uses a favourite Hindu colour – pink – and a favourite Hindu flower – the lotus blossom. Pink lotuses are also a speciality of Benares enamels (*121*). Lotuses are a symbol of good fortune, and this lotus blossom dhurrie was a special commission for a wedding ceremony. The central bright pink field is interspersed with pale blue blossoms; lime-green scrolling geometric leaves are arranged horizontally in a symmetrical and graduated manner to reach a central axis formed by a dark blue central blossom with chevron-type branches on either side, reminiscent of the pattern of the vertical axis of the Bikaner Central Jail carpet fragment. An endless repeat pattern is also found here, with the blossoms half rendered at the vertical edges of the dhurrie. The whole composition is enclosed within three borders and four guards. The dhurrie is inscribed at the top, 'M. T. KATHAWALA', probably the name of the person who commissioned it. The name itself is Gujarati, and means *jutewala*, or jute merchant. The bold and minimalist treatment of the dhurrie is very reminiscent of Chinese carpet design. This pronounced taste for Chinese decoration can also be seen in the embroidered borders of Parsee saris of the same period, suggesting that the patron M. T. Kathawala may have been a Parsee.

In another striking example from the same period (*122*) the overall composition of the dhurrie adheres closely to the traditional mirror-image and symmetrical arrangement. The pale blue main field contains a repeat pattern of alternating blue, red and white geometric vines, and red and white, cream, and blue and white blossoms. These reflect each other along a main axis composed of a burst *chahar bagh* (fourfold garden) medallion. The

120

Below Vine and Blossom dhurrie, Benares, *c.* 1920. 2.74 x 2.74m, 9 x 9ft. T. C. Goel/Samurai Collection.

121

Reverse of a square *bazuband* enamelled with a portrait of Ghazi-ud-din-Haidar (1814–27), king of Oudh (Lucknow) with pink enamel lotuses, Benares, early 19th century. Courtesy Christie's .

122

Large stylized geometric Vine and Blossom dhurrie,
Bikaner, c. 1910, 3.79 x 3.23m, 12ft 5in x 10ft 7in.
Courtesy David Black.

white border with its meandering stylized vines and blossoms is contained within two green guard stripes. Despite the understated design, this composition is well balanced; the colours and design, and in particular the border treatment are typical of Bikaner Jail where special commissions were all of very high quality. The eight pointed stars, symbols of spirituality and happiness, are often arranged in groups of eight.

Blossoms in Indian carpets and dhurries are often stylized and frequently resemble a lotus flower or bud. They are closely associated with deities in the Jain, Buddhist and Hindu pantheons.

Repeat Floral Design

Dhurries with a repeat floral pattern constitute a small group, and are mainly woven in a size suitable for a small room. The design descends from a large group of once very popular seventeenth-century Mughal carpets with a variety of alternating flowering plants, arranged in rows on a red ground, with an intricate border of scrolling vines and blossoms,[1] or alternating plants. Most of these carpets were produced in Lahore and were in the Jaipur collection, where some still remain.

The repeat floral pattern motif is quintessentially Indian, and is derived from block-printed Mughal textiles depicting the ubiquitous poppies, narcissi, lilies and other plants. The circulation of European (mainly Dutch and German) herbals in the sixteenth and seventeenth centuries, and the passion of Emperor Jahangir (1605–27) for botanical drawings have contributed to the popularity and dispersal of this particular design, which is found in book illuminations, borders and architecture.

The characteristics of the dhurrie illustrated (*123*) are the same as those of the carpet. Probably woven in Bikaner Jail in the 1920s, the dhurrie is reputed to have come from the Art Deco palace in Morvi, which it predates. The highly stylized alternating blue, pink and lime-green flowers in a vase are arranged on the natural ground in seven rows in a never-ending pattern. The whole

123

Section of a dhurrie with repeat floral design, Bikaner, c. 1920. 3.35 x 2.74m, 11 x 9ft. T. C. Goel/Samurai Collection.

124

Sample with a repeat flowering plant pattern,
Bikaner Central Jail, c. 1920.

is framed by an inner pink border with small geometric scrolling
vine and blossom and a wider blue outer border with stylized pale
pink scrolling vines and blossoms with yellow leaves. The choice of
colour and design is very reminiscent of the 1920s fashion for all
things Oriental, and provides a playful Art Deco feel. The stylized
vases look like inverted Chinese peasant hats, and the abstracted
geometric flowerheads echo the taste for flowers in vases found in
the so-called tutti frutti or *jardinière* brooches (*138*), designed by
Cartier and other European jewelers, and greatly favoured by the
Indian princes.

A sample from Bikaner Jail (*124*) shows a prison workshop
design that is also based on the repeating flowering plant pattern.
In this instance, the motif is a stylized plant on a cream ground
arranged in rows of alternating colours within a diamond border.
It is unusual, and recalls Agra and Amritsar carpets of the period.

125

Above Diamond brooch known as a *jardinière* or *tutti frutti*,
Van Cleef & Arpels, c. 1925, Paris. Courtesy Sotheby's.

126

Left A stylized floral design with figures, with a
traditional mirror-image and symmetrical composition
on a cream ground, Allahabad, c. 1930. 3.66 x 2.9m,
12ft x 9ft 6in. T. C. Goel/Samurai Collection,

Lattice and Blossom Design

The Lattice and Blossom motif is another great Indian classic dating back to the mid-seventeenth century. This highly decorative design was much favoured in Mughal India, appearing not only in carpets but also in metalwork; in architecture in *jalis*, ceilings (see *129*) and floor patterns; and in miniature paintings, particularly in border designs. Dhurrie weavers seem to have particularly favoured this design, of which many variations survive, and a more elaborate version of this particular pattern is found in Agra carpets of the nineteenth century (*128*).[2]

The most spectacular Lattice and Blossom dhurrie (*130*), probably a royal commission, originated in Lucknow where it was

127

Interior, London, with a Lattice and Blossom dhurrie, *c.* 1890. Private collection.

128

Opposite top Detail of a Lattice and Blossom Mughal carpet, northern India, 17th century.
Courtesy Christie's.

129

Opposite centre Detail of gilded ceiling, Jasha Mandir, Amber palace, Amber, Rajasthan. 17th century.

very likely woven in the local jail in the late nineteenth century. The overall design is the Lattice and Blossom motif formed by four white basins linked by water channels within a blue serrated *mahi* (fish) framework. This particular pattern was known in Persia, where lattices were used together with leaves. According to P. R. J. Ford's *Oriental Carpet Design* (1981): 'The leaf is regarded as a fish and the design is called *mahi*, meaning fish or the "fish in the pond" design.'[3] Here this is enclosed within another trellis of a larger basin in a form of a quatrefoil with smaller water channels, on a dark red ground – this quatrefoil pattern is used in Lucknow enamelwork as well. Manuel Keene, in a lecture on Indian enamelwork at the British Museum, May 2001, also attributed the quatrefoil design to Lucknow.[4] The main field is enclosed within an inner border of blue hook on a white ground, and an outer border of dark blue containing a stylized meandering scroll, white vine, and pale blue and red star-like blossom motif.

The Mughal flower-type carpets are profoundly Indian in style and inspiration. The region of Kashmir with its variety of flowers and plants so closely observed by the Mughal court artists, played an important role in the seventeenth century. The artists' naturalistic approach produces a contemplative effect. In the dhurries the pattern is more stylized and there is a greater emphasis on repetition. This rhythmic representation of flowers with alternating plants is found in all aspects of Mughal art.

130

Below Section of Lattice and Blossom dhurrie, Lucknow, *c.* 1890. 4.27 x 4.27m, 14ft x 14ft. Private collection.

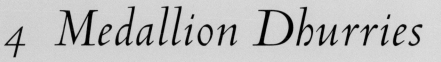

4 *Medallion Dhurries*

There are two major types of medallion dhurries. One has a never-ending, all-over repeat small medallion pattern, and the other has a central row of medallions or one large geometric medallion. The small repeat medallion motifs that are so popular in carpet and rug designs and look like a stylized flowerhead motif, are called *guls*, from the Persian word for 'flower'. They originate from a repeating design in the rugs of Central Asia, where each tribe has its own distinctive *gul* or set of *guls*. The earliest such pattern is found in the Pazyryk Carpet from around the fifth century BC. The central medallion motif is influenced by the Islamic art of the book – the medallion is often seen on the leather covers of the Qur'an, or in the illuminated margins of pages from the Qur'an.

As with so many other motifs from carpets that were reinterpreted by the Indian weaver/designer, medallions and *guls* were enthusiastically adopted and adapted for the dhurrie. The *guls* were derived from the popular lotus blossom motif, and the central medallion could be perceived as a variation on the mandala (a geometric design, based on a circle inside a square, with cosmic associations). The importance of the lotus is well documented in both Hindu and Buddhist worship, which explains the use of this pattern in rugs from Eastern Turkestan. By the late nineteenth century this was an exceedingly popular design whether in high-quality special commissions or in standard floor-coverings for the commercial market.

A rather similar repeat medallion pattern is also frequently seen in the painted decoration of walls and ceilings in India. Blue and white tiles, in the *chinoiserie* style, were not unusual in the palaces and forts in Rajasthan. A number of 18th-century

131

Interior of Naran Niwas Palace, Jaipur, with large *gul* dhurrie, *c.* 1880. T. C. Goel/ Samurai Collection.

132
Below Painted ceiling, Juna Mahal, Dungarpur, 18th century.

133
Right Detail of blue and white wallpainting, Samode Palace, Samode, Rajasthan, 19th century.

134
Centre right Chini Pol, or Chinese Gate, with blue and white tiles, Kishangarh, Rajasthan, 19th century.

135
Right Blue and white painted ceiling, Juna Mahal, Dungarpur, 18th century.

miniatures from Rajasthan depict scenes with blue and white tiled pavilions, probably Chinese exports, such as the Chini Pol, or Chinese gate, Kishangahr (*134*). The painting of walls and ceilings with imitation blue and white tiles was a cheap alternative, as in Samode Palace (*133*) or Juna Mahal (*135*). A variation on this theme, with terracotta as a third colour, is found in the ceiling decoration in Juna Mahal, Dungarpur (*132*). In a more naturalistic design, the white ceiling is painted with an overall blue cruciform pattern outlined in terracotta and darker blue, enclosing a terracotta lotus flower with leaves interspersed by sprigs of three flowers, two red and one blue, in a reciprocal geometric pattern (*132*).

The popularity of the medallion motif in the Deccan is also apparent in the painted. printed and resist-dyed cotton canopy, now in the Victoria and Albert Museum in London (*136*). Made in the early nineteenth century in the northern Deccan for a temple or shrine, the overall effect certainly derives from ceiling and floor decoration. The dynamic composition consists of rows of large medallions enclosing figures about a small medallion with a central figure, repeated in an endless pattern on a dark ground, and framed by a large border of alternating large and small medallions with figures. The scale and the densely filled ground create a dramatic effect.[1]

136

Section of cotton canopy, painted, printed and resist-dyed, northern Deccan, early 19th century. 2.64 x 2.16m, 8ft 8in x 7ft 1in. Victoria and Albert Museum, London.

Large Gul

There are a few large dhurries (I know of eight) with an overall repeating or alternating *gul* motif. The *gul* incorporates a flower-head (generally a lotus), a *bagh* (garden) or a strictly abstract design. These large *gul* dhurries seem to have been very popular, especially in the princely courts, as seen in such paintings as the watercolour of around 1805 by Sewak Ram (a Murshidabad artist at Patna), of dancers entertaining a nawab (*138*), and of which the dhurries illustrated overleaf (*142 & 143*) are important and fine examples.

Two samples from Bikaner Central Jail (see *137*) show how widespread was the preference for this semi-abstract floral motif. The standardization and simplification of the pattern, and the attempt to reproduce the pink – only terracotta is achieved – and blues of the Deccani dhurries prove the popularity of these flatweaves in northern India.

Among the most intriguing of all the large *gul* dhurries are those produced in the Deccan, most probably originating from the local jails and royal *karkhanas,* or workshops, and destined for palace use. By the time the British East India Company was in the ascendant in India in the eighteenth century, Deccani carpets had long been known for the originality of their designs and their distinctive colours, and these, too, are recognized features of the dhurries made in the Deccan in the nineteenth and early twentieth centuries.[2] The colours favoured by Deccani artists as

137

Above Gul or medallion sample, *c.* 1900, Bikaner Central Jail, Rajasthan.

138

Right Nautch girls and musicians entertaining a nawab, by Sewak Ram, pencil gouache and watercolour, Patna, *c.* 1805. Courtesy Eyre & Hobhouse Ltd.

described by Mark Zebrowski in *Deccani Painting* (1983)[3] – 'a particular lilac-pink, an inky blue and a salmon-red combined with rich and dark grounds' – are also a characteristic of Deccani dhurries, particularly a penchant for pinks. Even the otherwise rigid *gul* motif is transformed into a quintessentially Indian pattern with lotus flowers in the main *gul* motif and Mughal poppies in the borders. The fusion of Persian and Central Asian motifs is also noticeable in the interpretation of the pattern – the *gul* with its framing band of stylized *mahi* (fish) is used as an overall repeat.

This group of dhurries illustrates the magnificent variety that can be achieved within the confines of a rigid formal layout. The monumental design does not detract from an attention to detail in the inner decoration of the *guls* and the border, and the choice of colours is a vital element in producing a dramatic effect.

Comparison of this treatment of the classic *gul* with carpets from Khotan in Eastern Turkestan is also very revealing. Khotan carpets were held in Indian royal collections by the late nineteenth and early twentieth centuries – the period when these dhurries were made. The transformation of a geometric into a floral design is common to both, using the same system of rows of 'octafoils' with radiating flowerhead sprays linked by rosette medallions in the main field (*139*), and, on occasion, borders formed by double rows of rosettes or meandering vine and rosettes. Although the flatweave technique gives an angularity to the design, the overall similarities to the carpets are quite striking.

It is likely, however, that an even closer model was the classical Scrolling Vine and Blossom carpet design. The dhurries demonstrate the versatility of the design, although the composition, a never-ending repeat pattern within a large border, is very straightforward. The originality of the composition comes from the unusual use of strong contrasting colours and from a certain linear quality. In both the examples illustrated (*142 & 143*), the *gul* incorporates a large central lotus flower motif surrounded by four smaller ones within a strongly delineated medallion, out of which flow stylized leaves similar to those serrated leaves framing the central flower in the Scrolling Vine and Blossom motif. Even

139

Khotan carpet, with octafoil medallions enclosing flowerheads, *c.* 1900. 3.26 x 1.78m, 10ft 8in x 5ft 10 in. Courtesy Christie's.

the composition of the dhurries is similar to the Scrolling Vine and Blossom carpets, with rows of flower motifs cut at both end of the field suggesting infinite repetition, a common feature in Islamic carpet decoration. Both dhurrie and carpet are enclosed within a floral border: vine, serrated leaf and poppy pattern in the case of the dhurrie, forming a stylized palmette and vine border; and a palmette and continuous vine and serrated leaf border in the carpet. In *143* we have again a fusion of several classical motifs forming an original and quintessentially Indian composition. The combination of colours contributes to the dramatic effect of the composition: a dark ground with strong red-outlined blue *guls* within a contrasting dark red or pale blue border of distinctive Indian flowers.

In the other dhurrie (*142*), the ivory ground is packed with rows of repeated pink *guls*, outlined in blue, and incorporating a smaller ivory medallion, outlined in dark and pale blue and ochre. These are interspersed with another set of repeating motifs: a small polygonal *gul* radiating flowering branches and forming a reciprocal pattern within a pink border of small abstract motifs of leaf and blossom design, flanked by two narrow dark blue and green guard stripes on each side. The ingenuity of the design owes much to the choice of colours in an endless repeat pattern which could only originate from the Deccan. The success in turning an otherwise conventional motif into a flowing and original design, is due to a certain playfulness found in the dhurrie, in particular in the use of a 'burst *gul*' in the shape of a mini *bagh*, a garden, with flowering plants as the reciprocal motif. The individual and eccentric approach supports the Deccani attribution, and so does the angular meandering Vine and Blossom border, which relates closely to nineteenth-century carpets from Warangal (*144*), a carpet-weaving centre in the Deccan.[4] This dhurrie was probably woven in a local jail and is inscribed in Gujarati: 'Badruddin Muhammad Ali: Laila' (*142*).

A similar and even more elaborate dhurrie is the pale yellow, pink and blue version (*145*). It was probably woven in a royal workshop from the evidence of the ornate border, a design of blossoms and leaves arranged in a reciprocal scrolling vine motif, similar to the borders of Lattice and Blossom carpets (*144*) as

140 & 142

Below and opposite above Detail and section of large *gul* dhurrie with an ivory ground, Gujarati inscription, Deccan, late 19th century. 6.1 x 4.42m, 20ft x 14ft 6in. T. C. Goel/Samurai Collection.

141 & 143

Above and opposite below Detail and section of large *gul* dhurrie with dark blue ground, Deccan, late 19th century, 4.88 x 4.88m, 16 x 16ft, reputed to have been purchased from the palace in Bhopal, Madhya Pradesh. T. C. Goel/Samurai Collection.

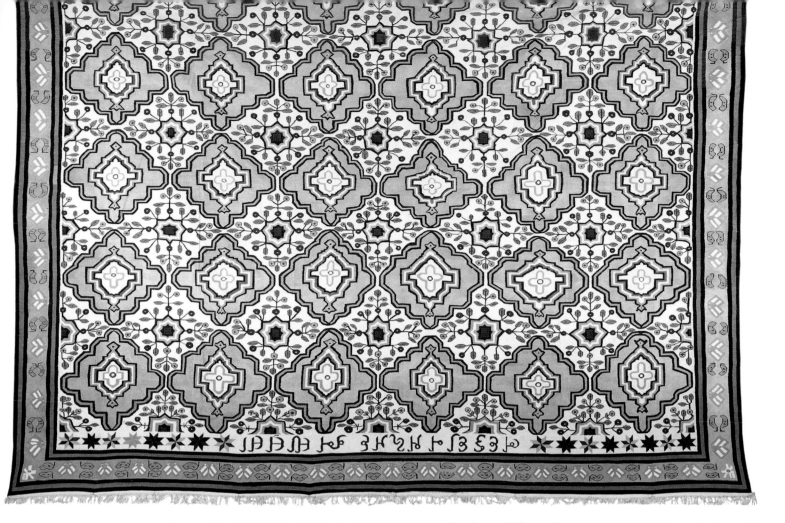

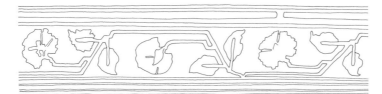

well as that of the blue *gul* dhurrie (*143*). An even more obvious similarity can be seen in the wonderful painted ceiling in the Lal Niwas in Bikaner Palace (*146*). The sophisticated Islamic pattern consists of interlaced white octagons, or medallions, outlined in gold, forming framed compartments painted with flowers, each octagon enclosing a stylized lotus flower on a red ground, or occasionally on a dark blue ground, forming another larger overall pattern. The delicacy of the ceiling, the subtle choice of colours and the marvellous execution is typical of the wallpaintings found in Bikaner Palace.

The monumental quality of the *gul* dhurries is typical of floor designs found in outdoor spaces in major Mughal buildings, such as the eighteenth-century brick floor design at Bibi Maqbara in Aurangabad, at a period when Aurangabad was part of the northern Deccan, and as a Mughal city had some very fine designs influenced by its Mughal heritage. The tradition of geometric floor patterns, however, derives from earlier Mughal buildings, such as the Taj Mahal, Agra, (1632–47). The Taj Mahal has a white marble floor with an overall octagonal interlaced motif, outlined in black, in a never-ending pattern, with half stylized lotuses at its extremities, within a plain border. There are

144

Left Drawing of Deccani carpet border with angular meandering flowers, Warangal, 19th century.

145

Below Section of large *gul* dhurrie with a pale yellow ground, inscribed F.A.B., Deccan, late 19th century, 5.8 x 5.64m, 19ft x 18ft 6in. Reputed to have come from the Nizam of Hyderabad's household. T. C. Goel/Samurai Collection.

146

Opposite top Detail of painted ceiling, the Lal Niwas, Bikaner Palace, built *c.* 1595.

147

Opposite centre Detail of silk double *ikat* sari, probably Patan, Gujarat, *c.* 1900. Victoria and Albert Museum, London.

148

Opposite below Sample with octagonal design, Bikaner Central Jail, *c.* 1920.

149

Opposite bottom Detail of sandstone floor, Taj Mahal (1632–47), Agra.

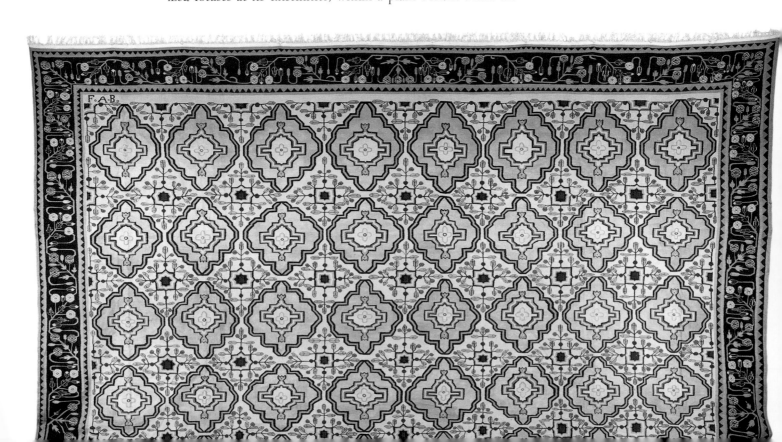

variations of this design in Lahore Red Fort which was also built in the seventeenth century. A version of the octagonal motif is also found in sandstone in the Taj Mahal (*149*) of which a woven dhurrie sample from Bikaner Central Jail is a good interpretation (*148*). The abstract designs and the endless permutations that can be achieved with reciprocal patterns were greatly to influence dhurrie designs, particularly geometric ones. The flatweave technique is, of course, well suited to geometric patterns, which were greatly favoured in most of the jail workshops, while curvilinear motifs, which required highly trained weavers and exceptional skills, were only made as special commissions.

A further important parallel is the pattern found in the popular double *ikat* (resist-dyed) *rumals* (kerchiefs) from the Deccan, and double *ikat* silk saris from Patan or Surat in Gujarat (*147*). In both, the strong Central Asian influence is apparent in the organization of the overall geometric design which was greatly favoured by the Muslim and Hindu communities.

Another large dhurrie with a burst *gul* design is reputed to have come from the palace in Indore, Madhya Pradesh (*150*). From its composition and choice of colours, it appears to have been woven in the Deccan. The pale blue field is decorated with an overall burst *gul* of yellow serrated leaves and stylized red poppies in a never ending pattern, within a large burgundy border of stylized blue vine, yellow serrated leaves and yellow and pink poppies. The contrast between the aquamarine blue of the ground and the dark red of the border is again typical of Deccani dhurries, confirming a particular fondness for unusual combinations and contrasts.

There is a group of large dhurries (*152*, for example) that follow the Turkoman (Central Asian) motif more faithfully, and which have a much simpler composition. The plain pale blue field is decorated with horizontal rows of hooked *guls* in a continuous pattern. Each *gul* is outlined in white, and divided into four dark blue compartments by two directional white arrows. The whole composition is enclosed in a dark blue border with a stylized white blossom and meander motif within identical smaller inner and outer borders of terracotta and white alternating cartouches. The blue and terracotta dhurries were both probably made in Jaipur, Rajasthan.[5]

The dhurrie illustrated here as *151* has a pattern loosely based on the *gul* motif, and belongs to this group of very large ornamental dhurries. This dhurrie is particularly interesting, as it uses the *bagh,* or garden motif, as a continuous pattern. The organization of the field into rows of square medallions formed by a basin and surrounded by fish, makes it an unusual variation on the classical *gul* design. The pale grey ground with its horizontal rows of olive-

150

Section of large 'burst' *gul* dhurrie, Deccan, late 19th century. 4.19 x 3.73m, 13ft 9in x 12ft 3in. T. C. Goel/ Samurai Collection.

green fish facing each other, framing a dark blue square divided in four light grey basins, is very different from the densely packed ground seen in the dhurries discussed earlier in this section. The simplification and abstraction of the design gives this dhurrie a certain primitive quality, which is even more enhanced by the two highly stylized borders of blossoms and meander.

151

Section of dhurrie with square medallions and fish, Bikaner, *c.* 1910. 4.57 x 4.27m, 15 x 14ft. T. C. Goel/Samurai Collection.

152

Section of large dhurrie with hooked *guls*, Jaipur, late 19th century, 5.8 x 4.3m, 19ft x 14ft 1in. Courtesy David Black.

153

Above Cotton appliqué wall hanging, Gujarat, early 20th century. 1.50 x 1.50m, 4ft 11in x 4ft 11in. Private collection.

154

Below Small *gul* bed dhurrie, Bikaner, early 20th century. 2.28 x 1.90m, 7ft 6in x 6ft 3in. Ganga Golden Jubilee Museum, Bikaner.

155

Right Small *gul* bed dhurrie, Bikaner, early 20th century. 2.28 x 1.90m, 7ft 6in x 6ft 3in. Private collection, Jaipur.

Small Gul

I know of only seven examples of the small *gul* dhurries. They have a distinctive composition that most resembles that of carpets, but with a slight variation in the colour scheme. They were all produced in Bikaner Central Jail. These are the most intricate dhurries produced in India, and the complexity of the design and the tremendous skill involved would certainly have taken a prisoner many years to perfect. The sophistication of the composition and the size of the dhurries must have made them among the most coveted bed dhurries. They were certainly all private commissions, and were made between 1900 and 1920, such as the example now at the Ganga Golden Jubilee Museum, in Bikaner (*154*) which was reproduced in colour in *Bikaner Golden Jubilee 1887–1937*.[6] The fine execution and the softness of the textile, which is cotton, is similar to that of the Sehne *kilims*, made of wool.[7] The rendering of the sunburst *gul* and the choice of colours bear a close resemblance to the Turkoman rugs, while the compartmentalization of the central field is reminiscent of Bergama-type rugs. The general format of the dhurrie, however, consists of a small central field and several borders, and is perhaps

influenced by appliqué and embroidered work – the almost
square shape of the dhurrie is similar to that of the silk embroidery or appliqué wallhangings found in Rajasthan and Gujarat
(153). There is a strong parallel in the general composition: the
division of the central field into compartments; a straightforward
horizontal and vertical division in the textile, and a similar but
more sophisticated approach in the dhurrie; the use of several
borders almost overshadowing the central field; finally, the use of
a stylized pattern and an abstract design.

156

Small *gul* bed dhurrie, Bikaner, early 20th century.
2.28 x1.9m, 7ft 6in x 6ft 3in. Courtesy David Black.

Painted ceiling (later restoration), Library (reputedly built by Dara Shikoh in the 17th century), Agra.

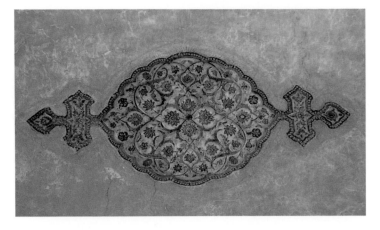

Central and Triple Medallion

There is a group of dhurrie designs that, although very varied, all focus on the centre of the field. They follow the classical central medallion motif, with or without a quarter medallion in each corner, as in the great sixteenth- and seventeenth-century Persian and Turkish carpets, such as the Ardebil carpet at the Victoria & Albert Museum in London, or the very popular export from Turkey, the Ushak medallion carpet.

The exceptionally large dhurries of this group were mostly commissioned for large dwellings, and were produced around 1900 in Bikaner Central Jail, as the sample from the jail indicates (*158*). Persian influence is well documented – 'Maharaja Ganga Singhji of Bikaner was known to have imported old Persian carpets to be used as models in his jail'[8] – and these dhurries are an interesting interpretation of this traditional pattern.

The dhurrie illustrated as *159* shows these typical characteristics. The ivory field with a scattering of geometric motifs, has a small mauve and yellow geometric central pole medallion with stepped terracotta spandrels, similar mauve and terracotta outer

158

Sample from Bikaner Central Jail.

159
Section of large dhurrie with central medallion, Bikaner, c. 1910, 5.64 x 5.03m, 18ft 6in x 16ft 6in. T. C. Goel/Samurai Collection.

160
Below Section of large dhurrie with triple medallion, Bikaner, c. 1920, 3.96 x 3.96m, 13 x 13ft. T. C. Goel/Samurai Collection.

spandrels within an ivory angular vine and palmette border. The whole is enclosed within three inner and four outer borders. This use of several contrasting borders to enlarge the dhurrie is a very effective contribution to the beauty and originality of a rather sparse design.

Another group of very large dhurries inspired by Persian designs are the triple medallion dhurries, of which one example is illustrated (*160*). The large pink field has a central green triple-hooked medallion motif, which has a cross design, with radiating stylized plants. The green smaller medallions on either side have a plainer cross motif. The central ground also has overall geometric and abstract plant forms with green and chequered spandrels,

within a main border of geometric blue and green blossom and serrated leaves on a pale pink ground. This is enclosed between a green and pink 'tooth' pattern and a green meandering vine on pink inner and outer borders. The design of the dhurrie is very similar to Qashga'i triple medallion carpets that were made in southern Persia, not only in the representation of hooked medallions but also in the meandering spandrel and the overall plantform designs.

There are other versions of this design with a purple-blue medallion on a cream ground. Bikaner seems to favour numerous elaborate borders contrasting with its rather plain field. These borders alternate between stripes and curvilinear motifs adding a certain rhythm to the overall composition.

This design exists in a larger version, and it seems to have been a popular design from Bikaner Jail. It is based on the classical medallion carpet format, with or without quadrants of a differently styled medallion in each corner. The two examples illustrated are based on a pattern characteristic of Heriz in north-west Persia. They even show other Heriz carpet characteristics, including the dominant central medallion with interesting details; the strong corner motifs with quarters not quite relating to the central medallion; the choice of colours, such as the light pink and the rosy brown shade; and the very individual treatment of plant forms.[9] Although both dhurries have these characteristics, they are totally different in treatment and effect.

The ivory field dhurrie (161) with overall polychrome and stylized flowerheads and rosy-brown central medallion with pendants, is strongly outlined and contains four large stylized blossoms radiating from a central square, with a rosy-brown meandering vine border within tooth and barber-pole-striped guards. It dates from the early twentieth century. This dhurrie corresponds directly to a sample found in Bikaner Central Jail (162) in which we can see a fragment of the outlined medallion with stylized plant forms, the polychrome stylized flowerheads in the field and the identical meandering vine border enclosed within tooth and barber-pole stripe guards.

The pale yellow central medallion dhurrie (163) is rather more subtle. It has an economy of design and an overall balance

between border and medallion lacking in the previous dhurrie, while the choice of colours indicates an earlier date, around 1900. Both dhurries belong to the more commercial production of the jail. Although elaborate in design, they lack the originality and attention to detail seen in other dhurries. They correspond to a humbler version of the large dhurries, and, in view of their size, were probably used as bed dhurries.

There are two highly stylized and very finely woven dhurries with a rather more unusual treatment of the central medallion motif (164 & 165). They were both produced in Bikaner[10] and portray characteristics similar to those described above. But the naive quality of the design and the mirror-image composition are a mark of their originality. The use of several borders, additional top and bottom stripes, known as the *patti*, and the fineness of the weaving indicate a special commission rather than a standard jail product.

The dhurrie illustrated as 167, an elegant and colourful stepped central medallion dhurrie, is again inspired by a combination of sources, and was probably made in the late nineteenth century. The madder field displays a blue stepped central medallion and blossoms, infinite repeat of rows of quatrefoil flowerheads, saffron and indigo meandering quatrefoil inner border, and an indigo, saffron and red trellised outer border. The dhurrie originates most probably from Lucknow where the quatrefoil pattern is often seen in enamelwork.[11] The combination of a classical rug design and a more 'Western' border is typical of rugs from Sehne in Iran of the nineteenth century, and the quatrefoil border is a direct copy of a popular Arts and Crafts motif often seen on carved furniture. The size and fineness of execution again recall the rugs made in Sehne, and their penchant for pale and dark blues with a variety of natural shades. The concept of the dhurrie and its colours, however, have become quintessentially Indian, creating a delicacy similar to that of some Indian textiles.

Another variety of the central and triple medallion motif can be seen in some dhurries that combine the motifs and colours of several different traditions. This synthesis contributes a very great deal to the richness of the dhurrie-weaving production in India.

161

Opposite above Dhurrie with central medallion, Bikaner, *c.* 1920. 2.13 x 1.3m, 7ft x 4ft 3in. T. C. Goel/Samurai Collection.

162

Opposite below Sample from Bikaner Central Jail.

163

Above Dhurrie with central medallion, Bikaner, *c.* 1900. 2.13 x 1.3m, 7ft x 4ft 3in. T. C. Goel/Samurai Collection.

164
Bed dhurrie with a central medallion enclosing
rosewater sprinklers, and flanked on each side by
flowering plants, in a mirror-image and symmetrical
composition, within several borders, Bikaner, c. 1900.
2.31 x 1.35m, 7ft 7in x 4ft 5in. Courtesy David Black.

165
Bed dhurrie with flowering plants, Bikaner, c. 1900,
2.08 x 1.23m, 6ft 8in x 4ft ½in. Courtesy David Black.

166
Dhurrie with central medallion dated 1901, decorated
with a semé of small feathered and stepped diamonds,
within a key border, Punjab. 4.93 x 2.95m, 16ft 2in x 9ft
8in. Courtesy David Black.

167
Dhurrie with stepped central medallion enclosing
flowerheads, Lucknow, c. 1890, 3.95 x 1.95m, 11ft 11½in
x 6ft 5in. Courtesy David Black.

168
Dhurrie with central medallion, Uttar Pradesh, *c.* 1890,
2.13 x 1.3m, 7ft x 4ft 3in. T. C. Goel/Samurai Collection.

A typical example of this combination of sources, creating a hybrid found only in the subcontinent, is the dhurrie illustrated as *168*, a variation on the Soumak rug design. Its palette of colours, however, is found in carpets from Eastern Turkestan.[12] The pale walnut field with its large blue *gul* central medallion, overall burst and hooked *guls*, stepped diamonds and stylized palmettes is enclosed within an S-motif and stylized cartouche border on a blue ground, a flowering vine border with a pale ginger ground and guard stripes. The overall composition and feel of this dhurrie captures the essence of Soumak rugs, in particular the central medallion with its semé (scattering) of motifs. There is even an attempt to include an ancient key motif found in Soumak rugs, but the pale colours, predominantly pale and dark blues with a variety of natural shades, are more reminiscent of rugs from Eastern Turkestan. The borders are also a rendering of motifs found in rugs from Khotan, including the stylized geometric and sea-wave border. The dhurrie probably originates from Uttar Pradesh where carpet production was very successful at the turn of the century, and carpets could be cheaply exported from there to the West.

The last example of this group combining several influences from different sources also relates to a group of tribal rugs, in particular flatweaves found in north-western or southern Persia, now Iran, although the design is very abstract (*169*). Different branches of migrating tribes often settle in different provinces, the Qashga'is of Fars in southern Iran, for instance, who are probably related to the Shahsavan and other Turkic-speaking tribes in north-west Iran.[13] The dazzling, uniform composition and the restricted palette of colours clearly have tribal origins. The strict use of browns, blues, and whites enhances the uniformity and repetitiveness found in the triple central diamond-shaped medallion pattern. The contrast between the large and bold central motif and the narrow and small borders with an indigo outer border, creates a tension in the composition that is typical of the folk quality of the dhurrie. The design also relates to appliqué work which is found particularly frequently in the north of India.

The originality of the dhurrie illustrated overleaf as *170* lies particularly in its square format, but also in its decoration –

169
Dhurrie with dazzling triple medallion, Punjab,
c. 1880, 4.2 x 1.93m, 13ft 9in x 6ft 4in. T. C. Goel/
Samurai Collection.

Square medallion dhurrie, Agra, late 19th century, 1.8 x 1.8m, 5ft 11in x 5ft 11in. Courtesy David Black.

flowing arabesques in the central field and meandering vines in its borders. This dhurrie bears a very close resemblance to an Agra carpet of *c.* 1880 (*171*). Common to both are polychrome palmettes, with scrolling leafy vines and an identical border of interlaced Vine and Blossom meander, one of which has completely faded in the dhurrie. The dhurrie's red central ground encloses flowing interlaced ivory arabesques with blue blossoms, outlining a large central medallion incorporating another smaller medallion of stylized dark blue, pale blue and ivory flower heads.

The whole is enclosed within an large ivory border with a dark blue meandering vine with red half blossoms interlaced with a now faded meander with pale blue half blossoms, between dark blue stripes. The dhurrie was most probably the product of an Agra carpet workshop, which in turn must have based its design on the inlaid marble tracery found on I'timad ad-Dawla's tomb nearby (*173*) of 1628. Steven Cohen, however, traces the design of the dhurrie to a foreign influence, either Persian or Turkish embroidery.[14] The parallel with embroidery, notably the fine embroidered covers from Central Asia, Persia and Turkey, is apparent in both the square shape of the dhurrie and the design of the medallion in the central field. These embroideries are generally elaborate, counted-stitch work, worked entirely according to free-drawn patterns. Here again the mandala design, a square containing a circle of vines, tendrils and blossoms, is apparent as is the influence of the large square woven Kashmir shawls, India's best known export in the nineteenth century.

More than all other dhurries, the medallion dhurries demonstrate the many and varied influences that played such an important role in the formation of the visual experience in the decorative arts of India.

171

Left Carpet, Agra, *c.* 1880, 5.04 x 5.16m, 16ft 7in x 16ft 11in. Courtesy Christie's.

172

Above Painted ceiling, Library (reputedly built by Dara Shikoh in the 17th century), Agra.

173

Bottom left Detail of marble and coloured stone inlay decoration, I'timad ad-Dawla's tomb, Agra, 1622–28.

5 Geometric Dhurries

Among the most popular dhurries, together with the striped, are those with geometric designs. The restrained use of colour and the balanced, unobtrusive composition explain their universal attraction. Geometric patterns form an important and integral part of both the Hindu and the Muslim artistic repertoire. It is the fundamental vocabulary of dhurrie designs. After the stripe, geometric motifs are easiest to learn in terms of technique, since they are based on counting warps and adding or removing wefts.

As with the striped dhurries, many geometric dhurries have a dual purpose. They serve as outdoor floor-coverings during religious festivals, large gatherings or encampments, and also replace carpets in spring and autumn when the marble or tile floors are still too cool to be left bare – the geometric designs were often adapted from the architectural decoration within the fort or palace, closely following the intricate patterns of walls, ceilings, pierced screens or floors.

Tile Pattern

The design of the tile dhurrie is determined by its function – a floor-covering that imitates tiles. Most of these tile motifs are based on floor designs and geometric patterns found in Hindu and Islamic ornamentation, and can be very complicated and very decorative.

The dhurrie illustrated overleaf as *175*, dating from the late nineteenth century, is a typical example of a tile pattern floor-covering. It combines the most appealing colours – indigo and white with a few terracotta highlights. The tile-pattern field is a combination of pale blue and white squares interspersed with dark indigo stepped crosses with inevitable changes in tone, or *abrash*,

174

Interior, Kanota Palace, Kanota with large geometric dhurrie, Ahmedabad, *c.* 1890. T. C. Goel/Samurai Collection.

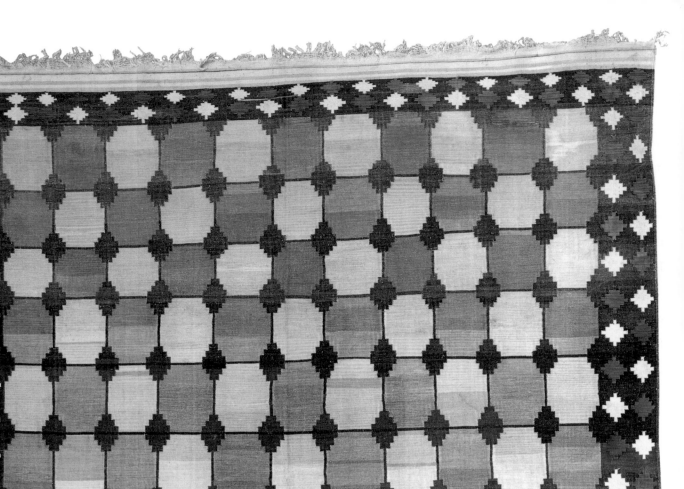

175
Above Tile dhurrie, Rajasthan, *c.* 1880. 5.77 x 4.83m,
18ft 11in x 15ft 10in. Courtesy David Black.

176
Opposite below Veranda, Darbargadh Palace, Morvi,
Gujarat, 19th century.

as the dyes are natural – this is a perfect example of the use of natural dyes with *abrash*. The whole is enclosed by a dark blue border with a double row of alternating white and terracotta stepped diamonds, and a blue and white striped *patti*. It was made in Rajasthan and used indoors as a floor-covering during the cool season.[1] A larger version of this dhurrie pattern was exhibited in 1851 as a wall-hanging in the Indian Pavilion at the Great Exhibition at Crystal Palace in London (see *21* in the Introduction).

Long narrow dhurries were commonly illustrated in miniatures. During the cool months, dhurries were laid down as floor-coverings in galleries outside the main rooms, for it was in these galleries that light handcrafts and repairs were often carried out. The tile design derived from such tiled verandas as those in the Darbargadh Palace, Morvi (*176*).

The dhurrie illustrated as *177* is an example of a tile pattern veranda dhurrie based on the same concept of a chequered grid. This dhurrie has pale blue tiles framed with terracotta and interspersed with dark and pale blue diamonds. This is enclosed in a terracotta border with an indigo key pattern creating a reciprocal effect often found in rugs. The coolness of the blue in contrast with the warmth of the terracotta colour creates an interesting and original feature. The overall balanced composition and design is a testimony to the sophistication of the designer/weaver.

The tile theme is seen in an equally sophisticated treatment in a room dhurrie (*181*). The pale blue field has rows of alternating dark blue and terracotta feathered diamonds in an infinite repeat pattern. The sides are lined by alternating and elongated feathered dark blue and terracotta half lozenges. All is enclosed by a dark blue border with a terracotta and pale blue zigzag meander with pale blue feathered diamonds. The whole composition creates a rather complex geometric illusion characteristic of tiled floor patterns.

177
Above Tile dhurrie, Gujarat, *c.* 1880. 6.40 x 2.29m, 21ft x 7ft 6in. T .C. Goel/Samurai Collection.

178

Left Begum of Nawab, Awadh School, 19th century.
Lucknow, Lucknow Museum.

179

Below Veranda tile dhurrie, Uttar Pradesh, mid-19th
century. 4.04 x 2.06, 13ft 3in x 6ft 9in. T. C. Goel/
Samurai Collection.

180

Opposite above Section of large tile dhurrie with
an overall blossom motif and key pattern border,
Uttar Pradesh, c. 1910. 4.1 x 3m, 13ft 5½in x 9ft 10in.
T. C. Goel/Samurai Collection.

181

Opposite below Section of room-size tile dhurrie
with feathered diamonds and zigzag meander border,
Rajasthan or Gujarat. c. 1890. 3.34 x 2.79m, 10ft 11½in
x 9ft 2in. T. C. Goel/Samurai Collection.

The veranda dhurrie illustrated below as *179*, dating from the
mid-nineteenth century, was produced in Uttar Pradesh where a
thriving carpet industry was long established. Despite its poor condition, is a very interesting example of an early floor design that
makes use of a blossom motif in an unusual way. The treatment of
the flower is very similar to the handling of a geometric pattern,
and the motif is juxtaposed and repeated endlessly with a smaller
cross motif in between, emphasizing the tile aspect of the design.
The border of the dhurrie is also treated as a tiled floor border
would be, with a sober blue diamond trellis on a terracotta ground.

A dhurrie with a similar pattern can be seen in a nineteenth-
century miniature in the Lucknow Museum depicting a lady sitting
on a veranda smoking a *huqqa* (*178*).

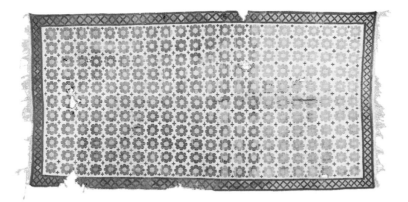

Stylized Lattice and Blossom

The semi-abstract Lattice and Blossom pattern dhurries illustrated here are based on the great classical Mughal carpet design, and the stylized geometric motifs make it an ideal alternative to the tile pattern dhurries. It is probably the most popular dhurrie throughout India. Woven in large or small versions, the Lattice and Blossom motif can be successfully adapted to the scale required.

Among the most splendid examples of this pattern is the dhurrie in Jodhpur Fort Palace, also known as Mehrangarh Fort, dating from the late nineteenth century and most probably woven in Bikaner Central Jail. The large pale blue field, now greatly faded, is decorated with a red lattice and white flattened and cross-shaped stylized poppies with red highlights. It is surrounded by a large red and indigo key border. The key motif is a very common choice of border design in jail products, and as a framing border it is an old pattern often used in Indian decoration, as in the early Buddhist paintings in Ajanta Cave 2 (185). There is a prison sample from Bikaner (183) which is a simpler version, but the royal commission, in view of its size and importance, dictates a more elaborate design, with an emphasis on scale and finish apparent in the edging of this repeat pattern. The scale and depth of colour of the border also creates an impact not found in the sample. The design of the dhurrie emulates some of the floor patterns found in rooms in the fort itself, such as the one illustrated here (186) which has a more elaborate Lattice and Blossom pattern with a lotus petal border.

The same pattern is used for other functional dhurries, such as the veranda dhurrie illustrated as 182. The bold use of indigos and reds is again very effective, creating a rhythm reflected in the pattern repeat. The border treatment is a reciprocal use of the

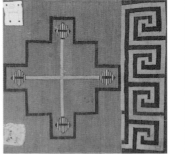

colour of the main field, the pale blue lattice with a red 'cross' design on an indigo ground. The contrast between the main ground and border of the dhurrie creates a visual richness highlighted further by the elongated and narrow shape of the dhurrie, made to fit a gallery or veranda.

A version of this popular motif is found in sample rolls in both Bikaner and Sabarmati Central Jails. It is again based on a trellis pattern with an abstracted lotus blossom, this time a staggered diamond enclosed within a key border (*184*). The lotus is

Section of large Lattice and Blossom dhurrie, Rajasthan, probably Bikaner, *c.* 1880. 3.9 x 3.58m, 13ft x 11ft 9in. T. C. Goel/Samurai Collection.

the most significant Hindu flower, as it is one of the symbols of Lakshmi, the goddess of plenty and fertility.

The dhurrie illustrated as the frontispiece to this chapter (*174*) demonstrates the dazzling effect of such a pattern when contrasting colours are used. The red and bright yellow ogival lattice runs all over the dark indigo field, interspersed with pale blue diamonds within the trellis design, enclosing a red staggered diamond. The whole composition is enclosed within a bright yellow stripe guard and a dark indigo and red key border. The play on dark and bright contrasts creates a jewel-like effect in the design, very reminiscent of Indian enamelwork or *bidri* ware, brass and silver inlaid into a dark zinc surface (*188*). There are several other versions of this pattern, but none of them conveys the same dramatic richness.

The lattice and plantain tree seems to have been a popular motif, as the numerous examples show (*190, 191*). It is again based on the classical seventeenth-century Mughal carpet design, but is reinterpreted to suit a flatweave, and incorporates local plants. It is mainly found in the sample rolls in Sabarmati Jail, Ahmedabad (*192*). The dhurries are standard size for large rooms. The example illustrated as *190* is particularly striking, because the

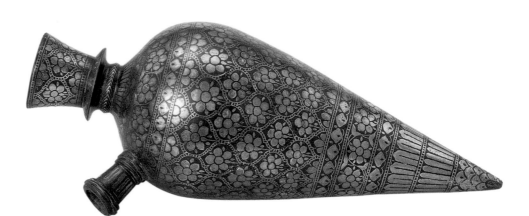

188
Bidri huqqa base, Deccan, early 19th century.
The Nasser D. Khalili Collection of Islamic Art.

189
Lattice and Blossom dhurrie, Punjab, *c.* 1890.
1.98 x 1.30m, 6ft 6in x 4ft 3in. T. C. Goel/Samurai
Collection.

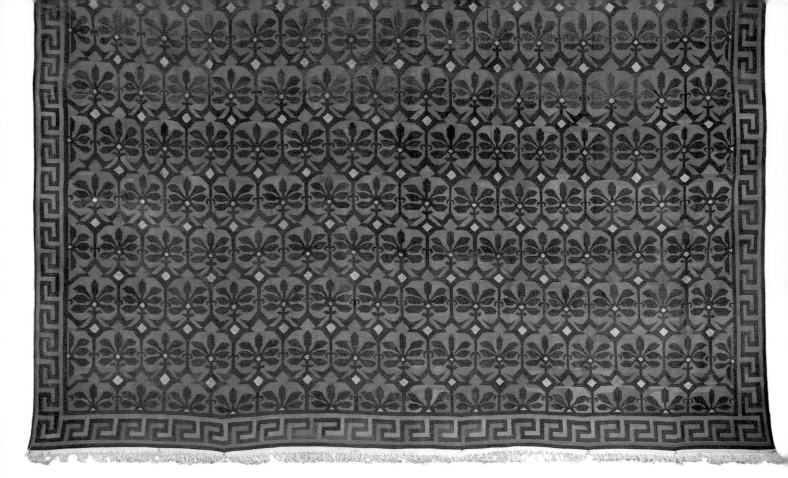

190

Above Section of lattice and plantain dhurrie,
Sabarmati Central Jail, Ahmedabad, *c.* 1890. 4.88 x
4.57m, 16 x 15ft. T. C. Goel/Samurai Collection.

191

Below Section of another lattice and plantain dhurrie,
Sabarmati Central Jail, Ahmedabad, *c.* 1900.
7.01 x 2.74m, 23 x 9ft. T. C. Goel/Samurai Collection.

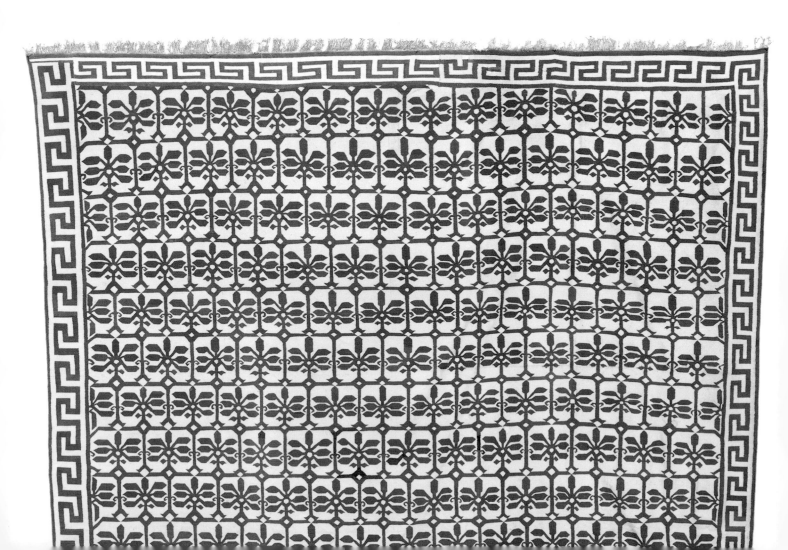

blue and red field is dramatically highlighted by a punctuation of yellow, whereas other versions are much more subdued in their choice of colour. The border is in keeping with the traditional and standard key pattern. The uniformity of the design makes it a more run-of-the-mill commission from a jail workshop. The plantain tree, a symbol of plenitude, is found outside every Indian home, and is often used as a decorative feature in miniatures.

Perhaps a more sophisticated treatment of the lattice design is the elaborate dhurrie illustrated as *193*, probably a private commission. The many colours used, the intricate pattern, with the depiction of buildings, and the complex border indicate further the special nature of the commission. The style of the dhurrie, the choice of colours and the narrative aspect of its design suggest that it is more likely to have been woven in Lucknow. There is a miniature rom Lucknow Museum showing Hazrat Amjad Ali Shah in a room with a Lattice and Blossom floor covering (*194*). The feathered trellis field, enclosing the spindly plant motif is very reminiscent of that in the miniature, and the colours are also similar. The buildings represented in the dhurrie seem to be both secular and religious, much like the buildings of Lucknow, such as the Imam-bara, and neoclassical buildings. Even the choice of colours – ochre, beige, walnut, terracotta, pale blue – are typical of the region.

A more usual version of the design can be seen in the standard jail dhurries and show an inventiveness in an otherwise repetitive pattern by creating a permutation of patterns both in the main field and border. The *svastika* dhurries (*197*) with cartouche borders, are a typical example of this. Most were woven in jails from Ahmedabad to Poona (Pune). Another example, most probably made in Sabarmati jail in Ahmedabad and dating from around 1900,[2] is the dhurrie for which the weaver has created an interesting composition by combining both the tile design and the Lattice and Blossom pattern in a medallion-style dhurrie (*200*).

Another design used for large room dhurries, of which there are samples in Sabarmati Jail that probably date from the 1920s (*195*), is the abstract version of the Lattice and Blossom motif

192

Sample from Sabarmati Central Jail, Ahmedabad.

193

Lattice and Blossom dhurrie, Lucknow, late 19th
century. 2.18 x 1.26m, 7ft 2in x 4ft 1½in. Courtesy
David Black.

194

Portrait of Hazrat Amjad Ali Shah, Awadh School,
late 19th century, Lucknow Museum.

(202). The dark red central field with its endless repeat pattern in indigo blue has a Lattice and Blossom design where the lattice element has been turned into a trellis of fish, or *mahi*, lending movement to the whole design, and has transformed the blossom into a burst four-petal flower deriving from the cruciform shape of four flowerheads found in some Agra carpets. The whole composition is enclosed within a dark blue and dark red key border. This combination of dark red and blue is dramatic, and the visual impact of the motif produces a psychedelic effect. This is a fine example of India's own interpretation of modern design.

The smaller version of this design in lighter tones (201) further strengthens the modernist approach of the weaver in both choice of colour and interpretation of design. The white *mahi* trellis of the main field, enclosing a pale yellow and indigo blossom, is framed by an indigo key and pale yellow border, and has a strong 1920s sophistication very much influenced by Western trends prevailing at the time in India.

198

Right Section of veranda Lattice and Blossom dhurrie with stepped diamonds and key border, Rajasthan, *c.* 1890. 6.01 x 1.83m, 20 x 6ft. T. C. Goel/Samurai Collection.

199

Below Section of lattice and Blossom dhurrie with stepped diamonds and cartouche border, Gujarat, *c.* 1890. 5.18 x 4.27m, 17 x 14ft. T. C. Goel/Samurai Collection.

200

Opposite left Lattice and Blossom bed dhurrie with alternating pale blue and indigo burst flowerheads, Ahmedabad, *c.* 1900. 2.13 x 1.22m, 7 x 4ft. T. C. Goel/Samurai Collection.

201

Opposite right Lattice and Blossom bed dhurrie with *mahi* motif, Bikaner, *c.* 1920. 2.13 x 1.22m, 7 x 4ft. T. C. Goel/Samurai Collection.

202

Opposite below Section of large Lattice and Blossom dhurrie with *mahi* motif, Bikaner, *c.* 1920. 3.66 x 2.13m, 12 x 7ft. T. C. Goel/Samurai Collection.

203
Above Jali design dhurrie, Bikaner, *c.* 1920, 3.50 x 3.50m,
11ft 5¾in, 11ft 5¾in. Courtesy C. John.

204
Opposite above Marble *jali*, Red Fort, Lahore, 17th
century.

205
Opposite below Fleur-de-lis dhurrie, Bikaner, *c.* 1920.
4.72 x 4.52m, 15ft 6in x 14ft 10in. T. C. Goel/Samurai
Collection.

Jali Pattern

Many geometric dhurries in palace *karkhanas* have a design that echoes the *jalis* of the palace itself. The *jali* pattern dhurries are deceptively plain, and illustrate how strong can be the impact of a simple geometric design. Its power is enhanced by the repetition of a simple motif, lending the over-all composition a minimalist, contemplative quality. The use of only two colours also contributes to this restrained approach, where less is more.

The dhurrie in blue and natural colours (203) is a perfect example of the simplicity and beauty of an architectural motif as applied to textiles. The marble decoration (204) that particularly favours this type of design is translated in the dhurrie by the use of an ivory colour for the ground, indigo-blue outline for the trellis and a key border motif, all of which lend a three-dimensional quality. Considering that this dhurrie is a late nineteenth-century production, this decorative concept is forward-looking and very modern. Bikaner Jail and most of the other jails in Rajasthan had this pattern in their sample rolls.

Modernist Designs

Dhurries with modernist designs are among the most surprising of the flatweaves. India attracted and courted most modern movements, and Art Deco palaces, such as those in Indore, Morvi and Jodhpur, were built complete with Art Deco furnishings. The influence of this new modernist trend is apparent in the design of certain dhurries.

The patrons of this fashion were undoubtedly the affluent, and these dhurries, mostly woven in the 1930s and 1940s, were destined for palaces and hillstation bungalows. They were produced in local jails, as a sample from Bikaner Central Jail shows. Most were large and used in main rooms. The colours tended to follow more modern conventions, some closely copying Western examples in their choice of design and colours, while others were a wild interpretation of a modern abstract design. This new outlook produced a number of dhurries that are most interesting.

The dhurrie illustrated on the previous page (205) is virtually a copy of a Chinese carpet. The design and colour are an example of the taste for *chinoiseries* in the 1920s in Europe,[3] and has a direct bearing on the production of this dhurrie in India. The stylized blossom design is a feeble attempt at the Blossom and Vase motif seen in the ornamental dhurrie (123) or at a fleur-de-lys design popular in both Bikaner and Sabarmati Jail productions; and yet still very effective in suggesting a certain spareness and delicacy associated with a trend towards pale colours and abstract designs in furnishings.

206

Section of a modernist dhurrie, Bikaner, *c.* 1930.
3.66 x 3.35m, 12 x 11ft. T. C. Goel/Samurai Collection.

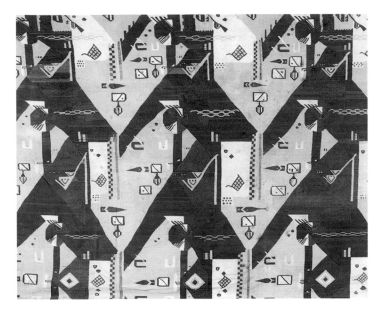

207

Left Detail of modernist dhurrie, Lucknow, *c.* 1930.
5.64 x 5.64m, 18ft 6in x 18ft 6in. T. C. Goel/Samurai
Collection.

208

Below Detail of modernist dhurrie, Uttar Pradesh,
c. 1930. 5.49 x 4.28m, 18 x 14ft. T. C. Goel/Samurai
Collection.

The royal blue, dark green, mauve, red and white dhurrie (*206*) was most probably woven in Bikaner Central Jail, as a sample there suggests, and is very closely based on designs produced by the modernist movement in Europe. The abstract, off-centre medallion-type motif with two geometric repeats in each corner, overspills into the borders. This breaking of boundaries complies with the breaking of convention within an organized format advocated and applied by the modernist movement. Although the dhurrie is an abstract and geometric design, it is perfectly legible and organized, and belongs to the central medallion type of dhurrie. It uses an old-fashioned concept in a new revolutionary language. The colour combination is unusual, even in a country renowned for its colour juxtapositions. The play of contrasting strong colours and dark and light shades also belongs to this modern decorative vocabulary. The effect produced is successful and exciting, conveying great enthusiasm and energy. It seems that many versions of this design were produced.

There is a category of dhurries with repeat motif pattern, and some employ an extraordinary interpretation of this classical design (*207*). The straw-yellow central field is dominated by a never-ending abstract dark green and dusky pink horse-and-rider motif arranged in columns, interspersed with floating abstract motifs, within an intricate abstract border. The effect is mesmerising and very difficult to read, and yet the format is to a certain degree quite conventional and follows the concept of the classical never-ending repeat pattern. The dhurrie was found in Simla and

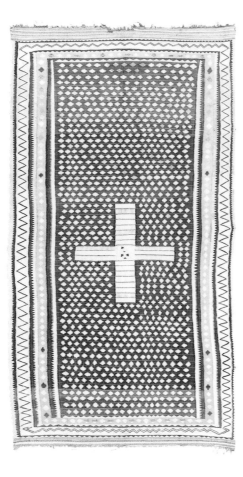

209

Chaupar bed dhurrie, Rajasthan, probably Bikaner,
c. 1890. 3.35 x 1.83m, 11 x 6ft. Private collection.

was probably woven in Lucknow – the evidence for this is a photograph of the prison shop in Lucknow with a similar dhurrie in the background. The subject matter, horses and riders, had a particular appeal to British patrons. As we have seen Lucknow had a tradition of representational design. According to K. J. Prasad, Lucknow Central Jail produced fine dhurries of 'fantastically dressed artillery men and pieces of cannon'.[4] Lucknow favoured rather dun colours, and the choice of colours is therefore also indicative of Lucknow as the centre of production. This dhurrie was certainly a special commission that would have required a cartoon design and a master weaver to guide the weaver in this intricate pattern.

The most abstract of the modernist dhurries has an angular design in mustard yellow and ecru on a blue mauve ground and border (208). It is practically impossible to read, and yet the choice of colours and the organization of space is very successful although simplified. The design is well balanced and yet not as sophisticated as the other dhurries illustrated. It was found in Nainital, another of the favoured hillstations in Uttar Pradesh, and was probably made in Lucknow Jail.

Patterns from Colourful Textiles

Block-printed and painted cottons, as well as Kashmir shawls were among India's most distinguished textile exports over the centuries. The fame of Indian craftsmanship was further acknowledged in the United States in the nineteenth century when international exhibitions, such as Philadelphia's Centennial Exhibition of 1876, displayed finely woven and embroidered Indian

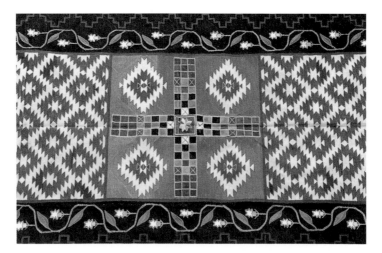

210

Detail of a *chaupar* veranda dhurrie, with staggered lattice and blossom field within a meandering vine and crenellated motif border, c. 1890, Rajasthan.
T. C. Goel/Samurai Collection.

textiles.[5] It is therefore not surprising that the successful textile industry should have an influence on dhurrie manufacture in India, particularly on the village weavers. The colourful turbans of the village men, for example, were a daily reminder of a rich and imaginative tradition, and had a strong bearing on some of the quainter dhurrie designs.

Among the most amusing dhurries are those based on the famous cross-shaped board game, or *chaupar*, a game similar to ludo (*209*). This is another example of a textile design derived from a floor pattern. *Chaupar* games drawn with rice paste on the floor are often seen in India. Embroidered and block-printed cotton versions are also found. The dhurrie illustrated as *210* has a complex design probably based on a textile piece with its elaborate diamond chequered field. The delicacy of the little yellow and blue diamonds and the overall effect is very reminiscent of *kathipa* embroidery, floss silk on cotton, found in Saurashtra, Gujarat, or of *phulkhari* ('flower work') from the Punjab.

There is a group of dhurries produced as bed dhurries by women in the Punjab, and these are therefore woven loosely with home-spun cotton. Their design is strongly based on a textile tradition, and the use of blue and white is very imaginative, entirely different from the small blue and white striped dhurries seen in Rajasthan and Gujarat. The Punjab and Sindh are renowned for their *khes*, shawls or covers, generally indigo and white cotton or cotton silk, with the most spectacular geometric designs (*211*), worn by the men. These were often woven in the jails in the nineteenth century.[6] Some of these dhurries are also influenced by the Punjab's *phulkhari* embroidery with its herringbone effect.[7] (*212*). A typical dhurrie is illustrated as *215*. The all-over indigo and white dazzling zigzag design has a contrasting large diamond-shaped motif at each end. Even the composition of the dhurrie with the emphasis on the two ends is reminiscent of shawl designs.

Bandhani is the Gujarati term for tie-dye. It is at its most sophisticated in Kutch, Gujarat, where the main centres are located, and in Sindh, Pakistan. The visual effect of *Bandhani* textiles varies from a simple dot pattern to a more complex medallion type motif. The dhurrie patterns derived from this popular tie-dye tradition are mainly produced in Rajasthan and Gujarat.

211

Top Detail of a *khes* shawl, Punjab, late 19th century. T. C. Goel/Samurai Collection.

212

Above Phulkari shawl embroidered with silk on cotton, western Punjab. Courtesy John Gillow.

213, 214 & 215
Village bed dhurries, Punjab, late 19th century.
2.13 x 1.22m, 7 x 4ft. T. C. Goel/Samurai Collection.

Village bed dhurries, Punjab, late 19th century.

216

Left Village striped bed dhurrie, with stepped
diamonds, combs and fish motifs within a crenellated
border and *patti*, Punjab, *c.* 1900. 2.08 x 1.08m, 6ft 10in
x 3ft 6½in. Courtesy David Black.

217

Above Village bed dhurrie, with bands of zigzag,
cartouche, chevron and tree of life motifs, Deccan,
c. 1900. 1.22 x 0.91m, 4 x 3ft. Private collection.

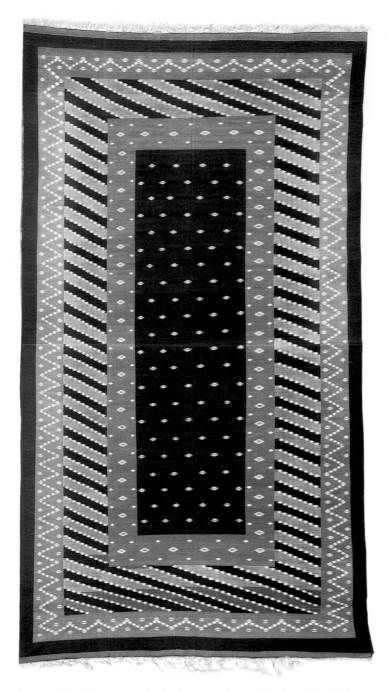

218

Festival dhurrie, Bikaner, c. 1880. 4.11 x 2.29m, 13ft 6in x 7ft 6in. T. C. Goel/Samurai Collection.

These dhurries are particularly attractive and original in design, such as the large dhurrie illustrated as *219*. The pale indigo field with alternating rows of yellow, pink, white and red feathered diamonds is enclosed within a large terracotta inner border with a feathered white zigzag and diamonds, and a dark indigo outer border with large terracotta and white feathered diamonds. The over-all multi-bordered composition has the same 'sparkling' effect as a Gujarati tie-dye wedding sari. Many of these dhurries were used for festivals (*218–220*).

The ability to interpret in so many different ways a popular motif inspired by the intricate patterns of life is a credit to the imagination and skill of the weaver/designer.

219

Opposite above Section of festival dhurrie, Bikaner, c. 1880. 5.03 x 3.2m, 16ft 6in x 10ft 6in. T. C. Goel/ Samurai Collection.

220

Opposite below Section of festival dhurrie, Bikaner, c. 1880. 3.28 x 2.44, 10ft 9in x 8ft. T. C. Goel/Samurai Collection.

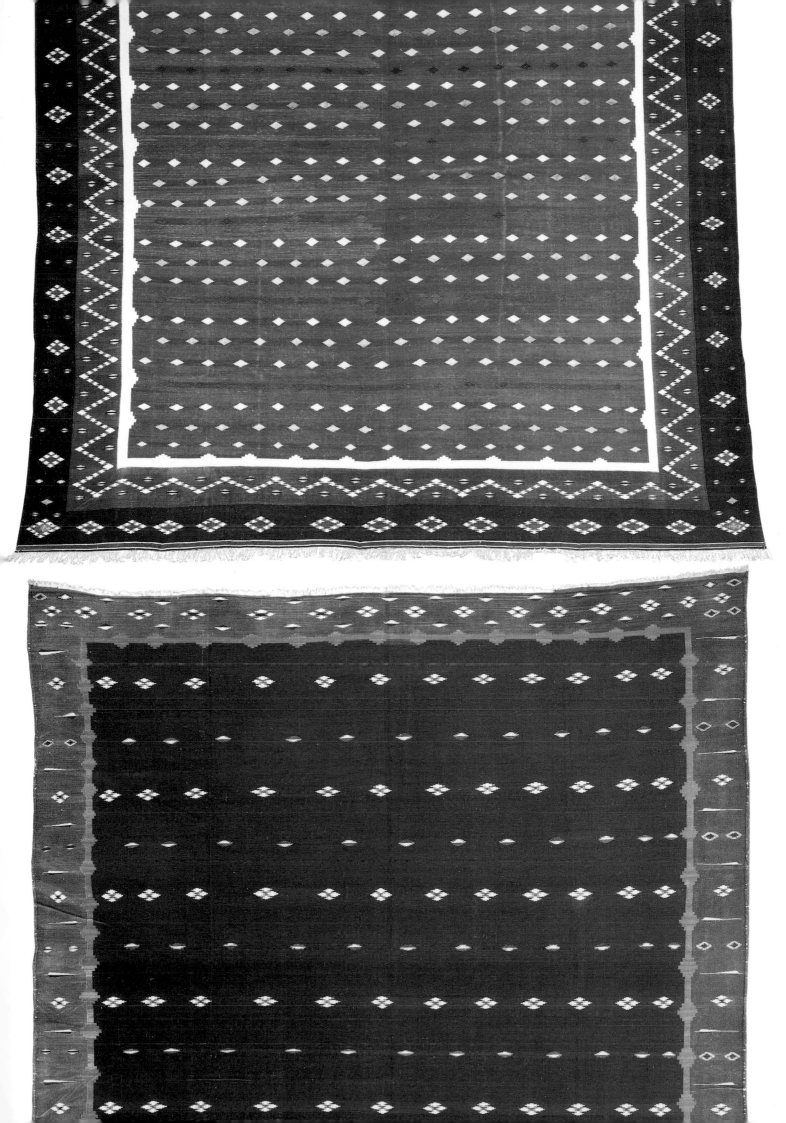

6 *Prayer Dhurries*

The concept of devotion in India finds its most important expression in religious practice. Hindus and Muslims follow different rules of worship. Hindus use individual *asans,* or mats, complying with the strict rule requiring a pure and undefiled single space for Hindu worship, while Muslim communal prayers necessitate multi-niche prayer mats, or *safs*, with pointed niches indicating the direction for prayers towards Mecca.[1] The dhurrie, a relatively superior mat, is an important feature in both Hindu and Muslim devotion.

Asans

For personal worship – *pujas* (homage to a god) at home – or yoga practice, Hindus make use of individual *asans,* or mats. These rectangular mats are often striped, a tradition that goes back to the striped tiger skins used by ascetics because they are thought to 'earth' cosmic energy during meditation. In Tibet, according to Lipton's *The Tiger Rugs of Tibet*, the rugs are often worn and marked in the centre because of 'the ritual performance in the course of meditation by the tantric disciples or ascetics who would have spent days on the same spot'.[2]

The Hindu rules for worship require that if an *asan* is soiled by someone else using the mat, it is to be destroyed and replaced by a new one. When this is not possible, the user is allowed to clean the soiled *asan* with water from a holy river, or a nearby tank or pond. If this is also impractical, the mat must be cleansed with water poured from a gold vessel, or water in which a gold ring or bracelet has been dipped to purify it.[3] This cleansing ritual and the fact that soiled mats are frequently disposed of has meant that few old dhurries that were used as *asans* have survived.

221

Interior, Somerset, England, with a monumental multi-niche prayer dhurrie.
Private collection.

Small village striped dhurries, Gujarat or Rajasthan,
c. 1880. 1.98 x 1.14m, 6ft 6in x 3ft 9in. T. C. Goel/
Samurai Collection.

The small striped dhurries 222 & 223 may very well have been
used as *asans*, especially as the preference for blue and white stripes
has a ritual significance. In Hindu culture *nila*, indigo, is not only
the colour of Krishna but is also 'likened to a rain-filled cloud'.[4]
The importance of water in dry, almost desert places, such as the
state of Rajasthan, is significant, and has led to worshippers and
weavers favouring this colour. A lighter shade of blue also used in
small striped dhurries is *hari nila*, the colour of the sky reflected in
the water.[5] These stripes are often likened to those in Muslim
prayer dhurries or *jainamaz*, but in the latter the stripes must form a
pointed niche to depict a mihrab. In south India, small striped
dhurries often use silk sparingly as highlights (224).

224

Small village striped dhurrie, south India probably
Madras, *c.* 1930. 2.29 x 1.37m, 7ft 6in x 4ft 6in.
T. C. Goel/Samurai Collection.

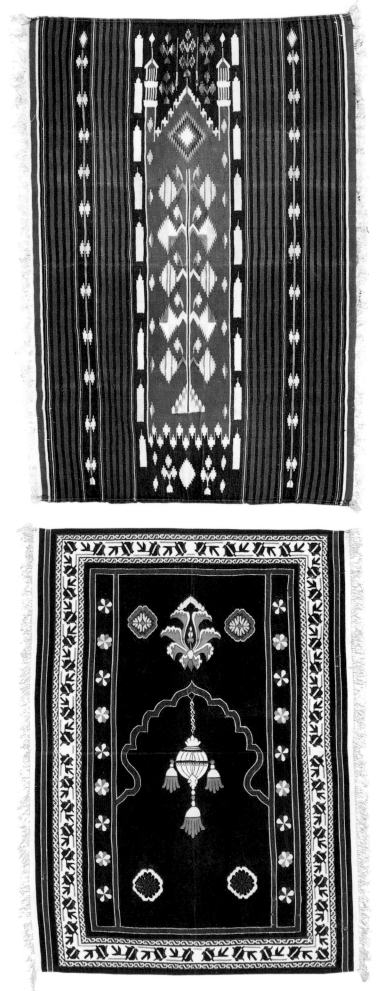

Jainamaz

Despite its restricted format, based on the pointed arch of the *mihrab*, the single-niche Muslim prayer dhurrie, or *jainamaz*, can be counted among the most colourful and original treatments of a functional dhurrie. It is interesting to observe the creativity of the weaver in embellishing a rather strict composition. I have tried to identify and attribute to a specific region, and on occasion to a specific sect, each design of the various prayer dhurries of India. But with time, the pattern has been repeated without any regard to the original intention. The Muslim prayer dhurrie lends itself to an easier classification.

According to Sir George Watt, the earliest documented single-niche prayer dhurrie was the one exhibited in Delhi in 1903, a cotton *jainamaz* from the Jami (mosque) in Bijapur, in the Deccan, which was loaned to the exhibition. In the catalogue Watt wrote that it was traditionally believed to have been left in the mosque by Aurangzeb after the conquest of Bijapur in 1686,[6] and goes on to describe its red central field with, 'hanging in the middle, a lamp symbolical of the faith', and as having been 'woven more like a tapestry than an ordinary dari'.[7] This *jainamaz* was most probably made locally, but at a much later date than that assumed by Watt.

There are several examples of prayer dhurries based on this design from Bijapur and from elsewhere in the Deccan.[8] The most distinguished of this particular design is the *jainamaz* (228), reputed to have been owned by the Nizam of Hyderabad, and dating from the late nineteenth century, very finely woven in pale pink, ecru and indigo silk and sadly now quite faded – pink is a favourite colour in the Deccan, as we have seen. The overall pattern relates closely to the design of the various arches found in the fif-teenth-century Langar-ki mosque in Gulbarga (227). The *mihrab* consists of a cusped pointed arch, with a lotus bud at the top and a full-blown lotus in each spandrel, framed by double sets of recesses. In the dhurrie this is translated into a cusped arch, with a split lotus at the top and a very faint full-blown lotus in each span-drel, framed by two sets of main borders, an inner plain border and an outer border with a stylized flowerhead motif.

The common prayer dhurries from the Deccan are among the most elaborate of *jainamaz* (225 & 229). Most have a purely linear

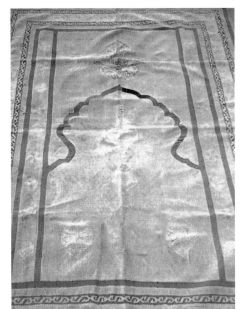

representation of a facade, a type of elevation particular to the
Deccan and found on the facades of tombs, mosques and even the
Char Minar Gateway, Hyderabad, of 1591, where the facade has a
pointed archway with numerous recesses, and the four minarets are
decorated with a chevron pattern and ascending arches. The effect
the dhurrie design is jewel-like as well as elaborate, and the combination of colours, which is traditional and possibly from Bijapur,
is very successful. The heavily outlined stripes in the *mihrabs* form
an important feature in these prayer dhurries: they are always seven
or nine in number. This could have a significance, and possibly
relates to the science of numbers and letters in '*Ilm al-Huruf*, a
branch of *Djafr* (a study of letters and numerology). For centuries
both Gulbarga and Bijapur were centres of Sufi activities – Ni'mat-
ullahi and Chishti respectively – and, according to Anne-Marie
Schimmel, the 'Deccani Sufis were among those who used the ver-
nacular language to preach their teaching of love and trust in
God',[9] so it is not surprising that some of their precepts are introduced into prayer dhurrie design. Furthermore, the monuments of
Bijapur are among the most important in India, displaying a
sophistication second only to those of Delhi. The elaborate architecture with its profusion of minarets, the treatment of
pendentives and ornamentation had a great influence on the design
of the prayer dhurries. This rich architecture was woven into
Deccani dhurries using a variety of colours and patterns,
creating a unique style very different from that of northern India.

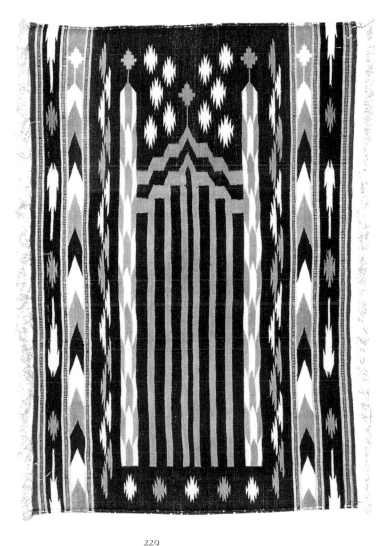

There is a group of Deccani prayer dhurries with an equal emphasis on the architectural, but presenting a rather more sedate interpretation. They rely much less on decoration and are easier to read. There is a certain sobriety in the depiction of the central narrow *mihrab* flanked on each side by two large minarets in red and blue with two white minarets at the back, all with pointed standards, and two stepped diamonds at the top and four at the base (*230*). The weave is very loose, and indicates a village production rather than that of a prison or a workshop. The pink version fits perfectly with Deccani taste and is marginally different in design, with an emphasis on the indentation at the base of the *mihrab* and lack of decoration (*232*). More minimalist in design, it is almost a transition to the interesting and more abstract design of a group of prayer dhurries, which relate to a much more restrained architecture and emphasize features of textile design as found in double *ikat* (resist-dye) weaves, such as *rumals* made in the Deccan (Muslim men's kerchiefs). The narrow indentation at the base of the *mihrab* stems from what is known as Hindu 'temple' design found in sari borders in central and south India (*231*).

The Punjab, as well known as the Deccan for its colourful designs, was particularly famous for its very fine cotton, especially in the regions of Multan and Bahawalpur. Both jails there still produce extremely fine dhurries with handspun cotton. There is a skilfully composed prayer dhurrie (*234*), unusually signed and dated 1305 (1887–88 AD). With its combination of colours and

230

Top Village *jainamaz*, Deccan, late 19th century. 1.04 x 0.61m, 3ft 5in x 2ft. T. C. Goel/Samurai Collection.

231

Above Village *jainamaz*, Deccan, late 19th century. 1.04 x 0.61m, 3ft 5in x 2ft. T. C. Goel/Samurai Collection.

232

Right Village *jainamaz*, Deccan, late 19th century. 1.04 x 0.91, 3ft 5in x 3ft. T. C. Goel/Samurai Collection.

architectural features, it is greatly influenced by local architecture, particularly the tiled facade of the seventeenth-century Wazir Khan Mosque in Lahore (233). The *Urdu* inscription is difficult to read, but suggests a private commission:

اونچئی (اونچائی ؟) سید شر بهردج (؟) کیا نام
خدم جسکا(؟) مریندل (؟ مزیندل ؟) پوره عیان
هدیه مصلی جونهرش (؟ چو مهرش) مسجد ...
اسلا (؟) بافنده ساکن ملتان ۱۳۰۵

'The eminent Sayyid Shir…with the name Kiya

Serving the renown[ed?] Marindel [Muzayyandel?], the son manifest

The gift of the prayer carpet…mosque…

…the weaver, the resident of Multan, 1305'[10]

233

Above Façade of Wazir Khan Mosque, Lahore, 17th century.

234

Left Jainamaz, signed and dated 1305 (AD 1887–88), probably Lahore. 1.83 x 1.22m, 6 x 4ft. Private collection.

235

Jainamaz, late 19th century, Bengal. 0.91 x 1.04m,
3ft x 3ft 5in. N. Afshar & A. Nanji Collection

بسم الله الرحمن الرحيم

'In the name of God, the Compassionate, the Merciful'

جناب نواب ناصر على مرزا بهادر دام اقباله

'His Excellency, Nawab Naser Ali Mirza Bahadur,
may his good fortune be everlasting'

Another colourful and interesting prayer dhurrie is illustrated as *235*. The composition is delightful, but lacks the sophistication and skill of *234*. Nevertheless, its folk qualities and bright colours contribute to its unique appeal. It is most probably a village production of the late nineteenth century, and may have been a gift, as it is inscribed in the sky in *Urdu* with a tribute to the recipient: 'His Excellency, Nawab Naser Ali Mirza Bahadur, may his good fortune be everlasting.' Another inscription is also found in the dome with the usual prelude to prayer: 'In the name of God, the Compassionate, the Merciful.'[11] It depicts the elevation of a mosque with minarets, arches and domes. The architectural features, with the distinctive difference in height between the central and flanking arches, the profusion of floral motifs above the arches and the detailed design of the minarets, are reminiscent of the pre-Mughal architecture of Bengal.

The Crafts Museum in Delhi has several prayer dhurries from Gujarat with the more common design of the *mihrab* flanked by two minarets within a row of stripes (*236–239*). The choice of colours — terracotta, red and purple — are typical of the region, which again owes much to its rich textile tradition and its vicinity to tribal artefacts.

236, 237, 238, & 239

Opposite Jainamaz, prayer dhurries, Gujarat, *c.* 1880.
61 x 91cm, 2 x 3ft. T. C. Goel/Samurai Collection.

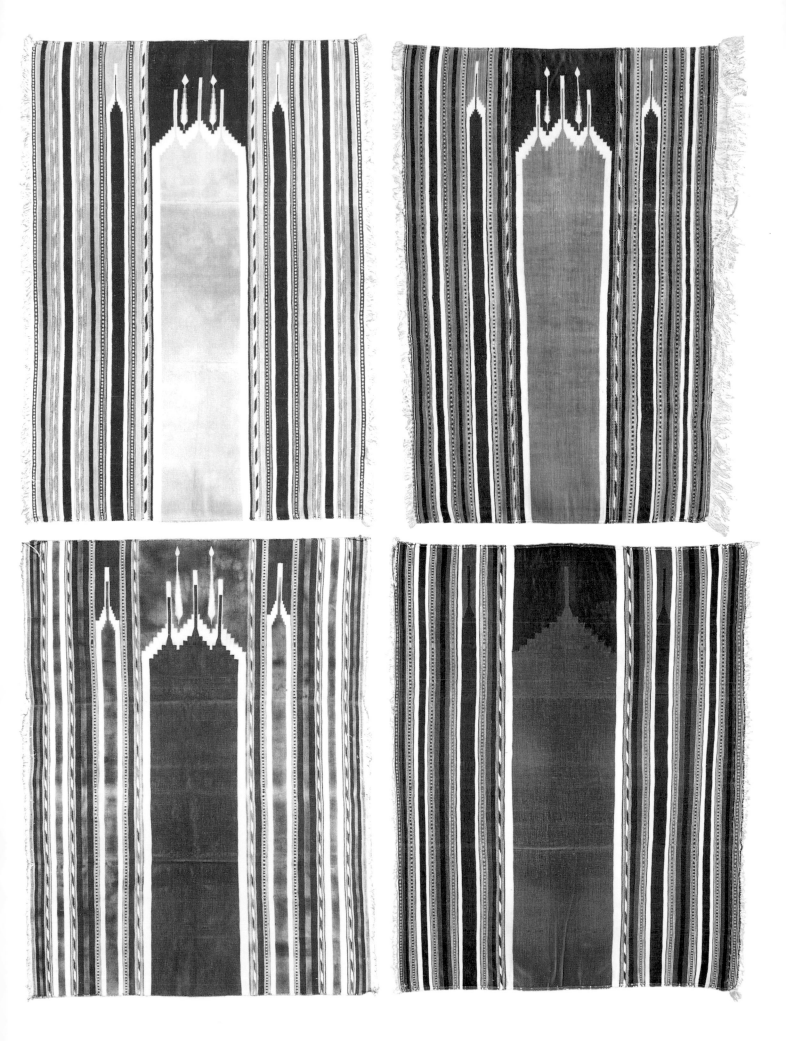

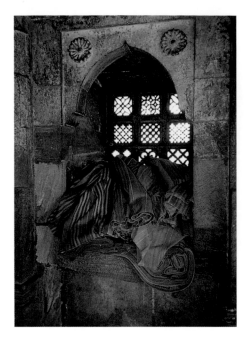

240

Storing *safs*, the multi-niche prayer dhurries, Jami Masjid, Ahmedabad.

Safs

The multi-niche prayer dhurries, or *safs,* further reflect the richness of Indian colour and design. This is apparent from north to south of the Indian subcontinent, with Rajasthan, Gujarat, Uttar Pradesh and particularly the Deccan (Bijapur and Warangal) producing some of the most colourful and original *safs*. The division of the marble floor of the mosque prayer hall into individual niches indicating the direction towards Mecca is unique to India (*241*). Decorative floors of the prayer hall would have most certainly determined the design of early multi-niche prayer dhurries, of which several fragments are known.[12]

In the nineteenth century most multi-niche prayer dhurries were commissioned by the mosques and were woven in local jails or *karkhanas* (workshops). The designs were generally reproductions of already existing and well known patterns. I have visited more than thirty mosques in the subcontinent, and whenever I asked to see the *farrashkhana* where the *safs* are housed, I was shown some old *safs* and was told that more often than not they were commissioned and produced in the local jail, and frequently copied the old pattern. On a couple of occasions, however, while visiting Baroda Jail (Gujarat) where the laundry section of the jail was cleaning the *safs* of the local mosque, I was able to examine the dhurries closely, and found a stamp indicating that they were the 'produce of Agra' (*23*). This led me to conclude that many of these multi-niche prayer dhurries of a standard design were very likely produced in workshops in Agra on a large commercial scale, and sold to mosques all over the country.

The most common design, found as far north as Multan in the Punjab (Pakistan) and practically all over India, are the striped multi-niche prayer dhurries (*243*), mainly produced in the workshops of Agra and Fatehpur Sikri, and widely copied elsewhere.

241

Marble floor, mosque, Taj Mahal, Agra, 1632–47.

These striped *safs* vary, from an elaborate depiction of a *mihrab* with diamond-shaped motifs in the niche, creating a jewel-like effect, to an almost abstract design of a greatly reduced *mihrab* with only the minarets to indicate its function and three diamond-shaped stars in the firmament. This play of dark and light colours and alternating wide and narrow stripes creates a rhythm reminiscent of the repetitive Sufi chants. The abstraction of the design, the repeated stripe and the contrast between the colours, with the intermittent punctuation of the diamond-shaped decoration, also contribute to the musical rhythm leading to spiritual enlightenment. The origin of the design must have stemmed from Ajmer in Rajasthan, where the Chishti order began in the subcontinent.[13] The Chishti mystics believed in *wahdat al-wujud*, the Unity of Being. For them, one of the ways to commune with God and be one with Him was through chanting, particularly the recitation aloud of the numerous names of Allah.[14] Devotion (*bakti*) through

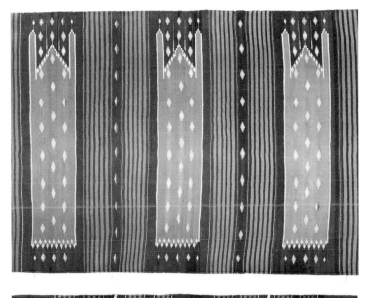

242

Detail of *saf*, Rajasthan, *c*. 1880. 1.45 x 8.99m, 4ft 9in x 29ft 6in. T. C. Goel/ Samurai Collection.

243

Detail of *saf*, Agra, *c*. 1900. 1.07 x 7.92m, 3ft 6in x 26ft. T. C. Goel/Samurai Collection.

music and rhythm also played an important role in the ritual observed by the mystics. The numbers of stripes and their division may have a similar correlation with musical notes as that of letters with numbers in the *'Ilm al-Huruf, the* science of letters. There is also a strong parallel here with the Ragamala cycle, which combines the arts of painting and music, and in which each note has a colour equivalent.[15] The Ragamala was originally a musical concept, and the introduction of colours, highly charged with emotions, highlighted their expressiveness.

The stripes of the multi-niche prayer dhurries, as in the Hindu *asans*, have a semi-magical function and are probably derived from their Hindu counterparts. Nothing is accidental in the arts of India, and the spiritual is always present, even if its original meaning and function have been lost. The collective memory and traditions always prevail or survive. These particular *safs* are found all over India and this is probably the most popular

244
Left Detail of monumental convoluted Tughra script, a Persian dedication inscription recording endowment by the court official Malik Hoshang, *idgah*, Jalor, Rajasthan, 14th century.

245
Below Section of monumental *saf* or multi-niche prayer dhurrie, Deccan, *c.* 1880. 2.51 x 6.71m, 8ft 3in x 22ft. T. C. Goel/Samurai Collection.

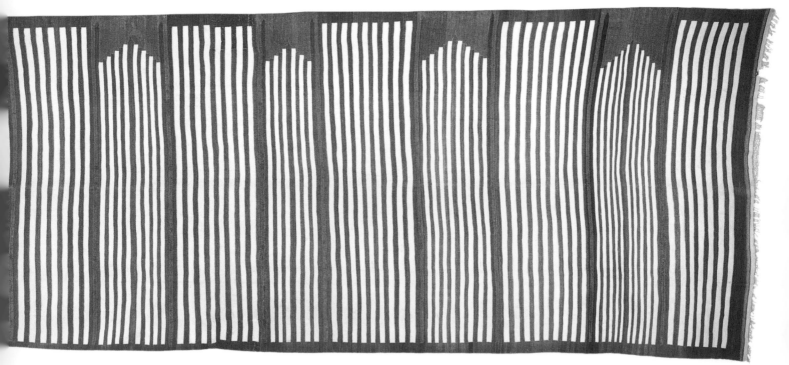

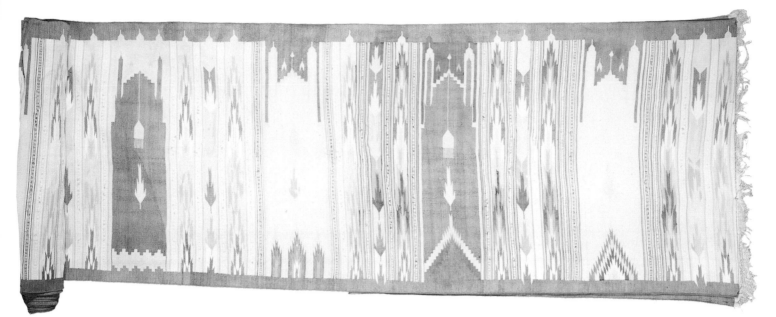

246

Section of *saf*, Deccan, *c.* 1900. 1.35 x 17.68m, 4ft 5in x 58ft. T. C. Goel/Samurai Collection.

and widespread design. The variety of colours is extensive and every combination is tried. They are the most commercial and common of all the dhurries.

Another group of extraordinary *safs*, originally commissioned for *idgah*, or large gatherings, and coming from Hyderabad, are the monumental striped multi-niche prayer dhurries (*245*). An *idgah* – as it is known in the Indian subcontinent, or *musalla* in Arabic – is in general 'the open space, usually outside a settlement, used during the *id al-kabir*, birthday of the Prophet, and *id al-fitr*, end of Ramadan, by the entire Muslim community',[16] and was usually situated at the gates of a city. The use of blue and white has a spiritual and mystical significance. It is closely linked to the state of elevation or *samà* reached in prayers. *Sama* in Arabic has a double meaning. It means the sky, the heavens, and also a state of religious elevation, heavenliness, close to the divine.[17] Most of the dhurries are not dark blue but a cerulean blue. The Deccan is renowned for its use of lyrical colours, of which pink is a great favourite, as is apparent in this large *saf*. It is significant that this *saf* and another like it (*221*) allegedly came from the Nizam's house-hold and were commissioned by him for such special occasions. Dedication inscriptions in *idgah* monuments are often in the monumental Tughra script, particular to India (*244*). The formulation of the letters and the rhythm implied is mirrored by the monumental *idgah safs*.

A further significant reason for the use of blue in prayer dhurries in general relates to the importance of water, especially

247

Below Section of *saf*, Bhopal, Madhya Pradesh, *c.* 1900.
1.22 x 8.23m, 4 x 27ft. T. C. Goel/Samurai Collection.

248

Bottom Section of *saf*, Rajasthan, *c.* 1880. 1.22 x 7.01m,
4 x 23ft. T. C. Goel/Samurai Collection.

rivers. 'Gardens underneath which rivers flow' is an expression often used to imply the 'bliss the faithful have to expect'. The Qur'an refers to the importance of rivers several times, in *sura* 47, for example:

> This is the similitude of Paradise
> which the god-fearing have been promised:
> therein are rivers of water unstalling,
> rivers of milk unchanging in flavour,
> and rivers of wine — a delight
> to the drinkers,
> rivers, too, of honey purified,
> and therein for them is every fruit
> and forgiveness from their Lord....[18]

Also popular in the Deccan are the very exuberant multi-coloured *safs*, with the characteristic 'Deccani' pink (*246*). The composition of this multi-niche prayer dhurrie is much more complex and less austere than the previous ones. It relates closely to the textiles found in this part of India, and, as with the *jainamaz* illustrated as *231*, the temple design at the base of the *mihrabs* and the strong colours are reminiscent of bright south Indian saris with temple-design borders. The jaggedness of the striped design between the niches is a reminder of the *ikat* design of the *rumals* of the Deccan, but also of silk weaves in general. The vibrancy of the design and the choice of colours make this dhurrie a truly exciting combination of the Hindu and Muslim artistic vocabularies.

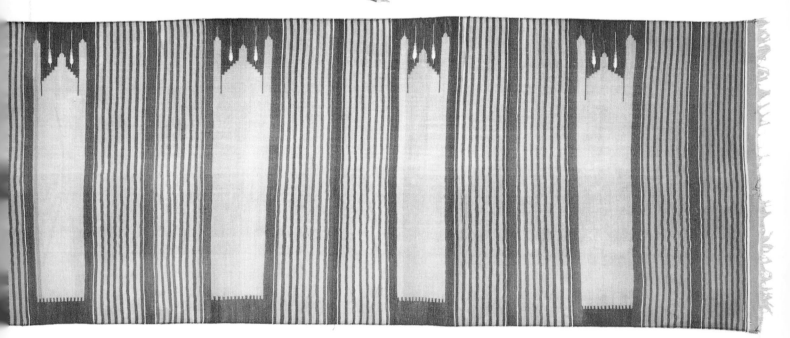

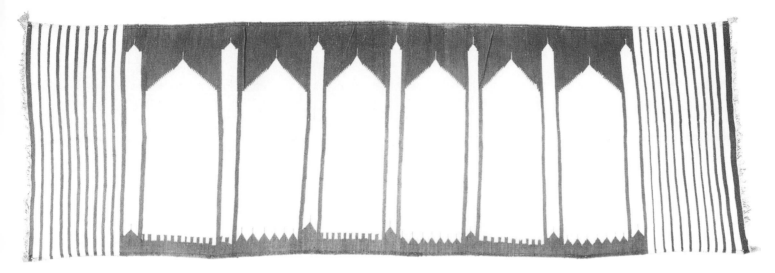

The other most popular design, faithfully copying the marble floor design found in prayer halls, are the two-toned *safs*. They are among the most aesthetically pleasing dhurries because of the simplicity and purity of the pattern. Blue and white are again the most favoured colours, as in the unusual *saf* in the Atala Mosque in Jaunpur in Uttar Pradesh (250). This is woven all in one piece, not in the standard design of single horizontal bands but in vertical and horizontal rows, reminiscent of a marble floor arrangement (249). Rajasthan and Uttar Pradesh seem to have preferred blue and white, the main difference being the composition. Rajasthani *safs* favour perhaps a more rhythmic pattern (248) punctuated by a predilection for the stripe, and those from Uttar Pradesh[19] prefer a plainer almost abstract pattern (250) with large areas of colour giving them a more sedate feel.

This fundamental difference in composition from state to state also applies to other *safs*. Madhya Pradesh favours delicate mauves and pale cyclamen hues in again a very simple almost abstract style (247) while Rajasthan prefers more conventional colours such as indigo and white, indigo and pale blue, or terracotta and blue with an emphasis still on the vertical stripe as seen in jail samples from Jodhpur, Jaipur and Bikaner.

Although weavers in both states use a stepped mihrab with *tùbà* trees at the top, the difference is in the arrangement and the colours. The composition of *safs* in Rajasthan and the emphasis on stripes is evidently influenced by the *safs* produced in Ajmer, Rajasthan, where the Chishti order prevails. Indigo, white and terracotta in Chishti shrines accords with the Chishti aim 'to develop river-like generosity, sun-like affection and earth-like hospitality'.[20]

249
Top Village *saf*, Rajasthan, *c.* 1880. 1.22 x 3.58m,
4ft x 11ft 9in. Private collection.

250
Above Detail of *saf*, *c.* 1880, Atala Mosque, Jaunpur.

Detail of a village *saf* or multi-niche prayer dhurrie, Deccan, *c.* 1880. 1.22 x 7.32m, 4 x 24ft. T. C. Goel/ Samurai Collection.

Gujarat seems to have cultivated a wholly different style despite the popularity of the ubiquitous Agra striped *saf*. Local styles flourished, as in the *saf* from Jamnagar (illustrated as *253*), probably produced in Surat,[21] in dark green, red and yellow with a design very reminiscent of Gujarati appliqué textiles. The contrast between the green and the red, and the stepped diamonds and chevron motif in the columns of the *mihrab* are similar to the colour contrasts and stepped diamonds of mirror appliqué in the textiles. The chevrons, although based on an architectural vocabulary, are also reminiscent of *ikat* weaving in the saris from Patola, and the vibrant colours are typical of Gujarat.

These attributes also apply to the *saf* inscribed Jami Masjid Baroda (*252*). It is interesting that an ordinary mosque would use both a standard commercial design from Agra (illustrated as *23*), and an elaborate dhurrie, an endowment or a gift.

The dhurries ilustrated as *252 & 253* were probably both made in the early part of the twentieth century, and display the rich eclectic tradition of textile designs in Gujarat. The decorative effect of *252* is almost abstracted, and the emphasis on design is greater than in the more traditional prayer rugs, so that the result is far more complex. This 'psychedelic' style, dictated by the choice of colours, is almost impossible to read. While *safs* from the Deccan are more lyrical, easier to read and relatively sedate, the Gujarati dhurries include a whole array of motifs, although cohesively put together. They are characteristic of the west coast of India where the decorative vocabulary is extremely rich and combines many influences.

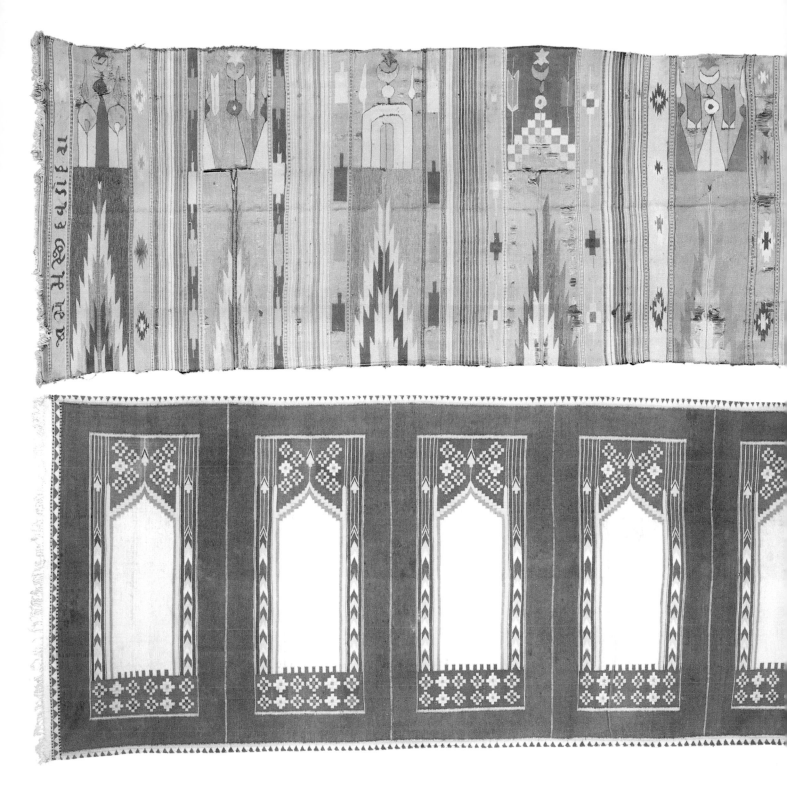

252

Top Detail of *saf*, inscribed Jami Masjid Baroda, Gujarat, *c.* 1910. 1.22 x 5.97m, 4ft x 19ft 7in. T. C. Goel/Samurai Collection.

253

Above Detail of *saf*, multi-niche prayer dhurrie, Gujarat, *c.* 1920. 1.22 x 7.32m, 4 x 24ft. T. C. Goel/Samurai Collection.

Conclusion

It is very difficult to get a precise and definite picture of old Indian dhurries because of the patchy nature of the evidence and the chequered history of the dhurrie. There is no doubt, however, that the dhurrie deserves its place in the history of the arts and crafts of the Indian subcontinent because of its originality and unique nature. Intricate patterns and original designs have shone through. The Indian dhurrie is no longer synonymous only with the striped flatweave – the nature of the commission still dictates the quality of the finished product. Weavers are sensitive to the other visual arts, and are skilful at adapting the overall design to the materials used. They are aware of designs appearing in other arts, observe their own surroundings and are familiar with the long-established tradition in India of renewing and adapting patterns by copying old ones. The themes that concern them stem from the rich repertoire of the Buddhist, Hindu and Muslim culture that surrounds them. The interaction of ideas, rituals and, above all, forms of representation has led to a fusion of styles unparalleled elsewhere. Even foreign influences have been absorbed and transformed into a unique Indian style.

Regional characteristics and centres of excellence emerge from this study. The Deccan, long neglected, is now widely recognized as a centre of excellence. Deccani dhurries, like the Deccani carpets, can be identified by their individuality and their use of whimsical colours. Like the architecture and painting schools of the region, the dhurries have a distinctive style which proved extremely popular all over the country.

Bikaner in Rajasthan, a famous carpet- and dhurrie-weaving region, emerges as the main centre in the north. Famous for its wool, its handspun cotton and skilled workers, Bikaner dictates the trend in sophisticated design. From the traditional copies of old carpet patterns to a more modernist approach, the weavers in the Central Jail in Bikaner could tackle any design. Rajasthan, and particularly the region of Ajmer, generally favours blue and white stripes, but dhurries from Bikaner are certainly the finest ever produced.

The Punjab produces very fine cotton which contributes to the quality of its handspun cotton yarns. The individual character of its designs and its successful cottage industry makes it unique in the production of folk art in India.

The commercial workshops of Agra specialized in the production of individual prayer dhurries and striped *safs*. These were sold all over the subcontinent, and are still to be found in storerooms and mosques.

Gujarat and Sindh had two main influences, the woollen artefacts of neighbouring tribes and their own colourful textile industry. Gujarat dhurries favour natural, camel and terracotta tones, with the occasional weft float brocade technique, or designs that derive from *ikat* weave and appliqué embroidery.

The south, represented by Madras, remains traditional with its use of stripes, but the use of strong warm colours and silk inclusions are characteristics specific to the region.

The jails have a standard production which favours geometric designs taken from the sample rolls common to most of them. It is therefore very difficult to be precise in the attribution of a standard dhurrie, although when it is a special commission the regional characteristics are very apparent. Local architecture, textile traditions and choice of colours can be determining factors.

A revival of the industry and an attempt to rehabilitate the aesthetic aspect of the dhurrie began in the 1980s. Vegetable dyes are more in demand for use in India's textile industries, which has led to the revival of a technique that had almost disappeared. An increasing demand from the West for soft, understated colours has encouraged local cottage industries to produce modern dhurries with natural dyes. The result is successful, but lacks the originality and punch of the old dhurries. The Indian delight in dramatic colour has been to a certain degree sacrificed for the Western taste for more subdued pastels. Interior designers in the West used to be the main purchasers of old dhurries. The rehabilitation of old dhurries, however, has begun, and there are now serious attempts by local dealers to locate and acquire surviving examples of the colourful and imaginative art of Indian dhurrie-weavers.

Notes

In the Notes short titles are given for publications listed in full in the Select Bibliography.

Introduction pp. 6–37

1 Vrata or ritual protection, see Gray (ed.), *The Arts of India*, p. 136.
2 See Huyler, *Painted Prayers*, p. 19.
3 Ibid, p. 16.
4 See Cohen, 'Indian Subcontinent: Carpets' in Grove's *The Dictionary of Art*, J. Turner (ed.), vol. 15, p. 681.
5 Huyler, *Painted Prayers*, p. 76.
6 Ibid.
7 See 'Utensils' in *Cooking for the Gods, The Art of Home Ritual in Bengal*, Ghosh et al.
8 See Cooper and Gillow, *Arts and Crafts of India*, p. 135.
9 See Lipton (ed.), *The Tiger Rugs of Tibet*, pp. 10–12.
10 See Welch, *India: Art and Culture*, p. 138.
11 See Danielou, *Hindu Polytheism*, p. 216.
12 Birdwood, *The Arts of India*, p. 285.
13 Detailed inventory record N.vii.3; see A. Stein in *Ancient Khotan*, vol. II, pp. 333–334.
14 Behl, *The Ajanta Caves*, p. 99.
15 Ahuja, *Dhurrie*, p. 39.
16 Ajanta, wall paintings Cave I.
17 *Padshahnama*, Folio 214B, Royal Library, Windsor Castle.
18 Calico Museum of Textiles, Ahmedabad, Gujarat, Accession No. 1423.
19 Kalat Bhavan Museum in Benares, Accession No. 9973.
20 See Terry, *A Voyage to East India*, London, 1777, quoted in Cohen *The Unappreciated Dhurrie*, p. 7.
21 Arthur Coke Burnell (ed.), *The Voyage of John Huyghen van Linshoten to the East Indies*, pp. 60–61.
22 I am indebted to Manijeh Bayani-Wolpert, Robert Skelton and Michael Rogers for their help in this matter.
23 *Imperial Gazetteer of India*, 'Rajputana', Calcutta, 1908, pp. 56 and 492.
24 Mukharji, *Art Manufactures of India*.
25 Birdwood, *The Arts of India*, p. 247.
26 Ibid, p. 257.
27 Ibid.
28 Ibid.
29 Mukerji, *A Monograph on Carpet Weaving in Bengal*.
30 See Sahai in 'Carpet Weaving at Jaipur Jail: The Early Years', p. 17.
31 See Hakoor Futeh Singh Chanpawat, *Brief History of Jeypore*.
32 Sahai, 'Carpet Weaving at Jaipur Jail: The Early Years', p. 20.
33 See 'Notes on Jaipur', Lt. Col. Stevens, Jaipur, 1909; 2nd edn, October 1916, p. 40.
34 Ibid.
35 Sahai, 'Carpet Weaving at Jaipur Jail: The Early Years', p. 22.
36 Ibid, p. 23.
37 See 'Jail Chapter XI' by Lt. Col. J. P. Huban in *The Jaipur Album: or All About Jaipur*, Jain and Jain (eds).
38 Ibid, Chapter XI, p. 3.
39 *Report on the Administration of the Bikaner State 1893–94*, p. 127.
40 Watt, *Indian Art at Delhi 1903*, p. 446.
41 Ahuja, *Dhurrie*, p. 65.
42 See Sahai, 'Carpet Weaving at Jaipur Jail: The Early Years', p. 20.
43 Ahuja, *Dhurrie*, p. 64.
44 Strabo in Birdwood, *The Arts of India*.
45 See Gillow and Barnard, *Traditional Indian Textiles*, p. 7.
46 Ibid.
47 See Birdwood, *The Arts of India*, pp. 234–35.
48 Ibid, p. 244.
49 See Cohen in *Silk and Stone: The Third Hali Annual*, pp. 239–40.

Chapter 1 Striped Dhurries pp. 38–51

1 The classic seat cover of the yogi, see Zimmer, *Myths and Symbols in Indian Art and Civilisation*, p. 198.
2 I am indebted to Manijeh Bayani-Wolpert for reading the inscription and identifying the donor as Mustawfi al-Mamalik. 'It is the official title of the Minister of Finance. A few can be listed, but none are recorded as having a particular connection with Shah Nimatullah. The other titles used in the inscriptions are those popular during Nassir al-Din Shah's reign. This would limit the search to Mirza Hassan 1780–1845, who received his post in 1835–36, and his son Mirza Yusif 1812–1885. He is recorded as being interested in Sufism particularly that of Baba Qalandar Shah who died 1860–61.'
3 See Soustiel, *La Céramique Islamique*, p. 238.
4 See 'A Group of Entertainers', in *Wonders of a Golden Age*, Goswamy and Fischer, p. 215.
5 See Schimmel, 'The Celestial Garden', p. 18.
6 In 'Kulliyat-i Ghalib. IV. Ghazaliyat-i Farisi', ibid, p. 19. The poet Minza Asadullah Khan Ghalib, 1797–1869, wrote both in Urdu and Persian. He was commissioned by the last Mughal Emperor Bahadur Shah II to write a history of the Mughals in Persian.

Chapter 2 Pictorial Dhurries pp. 52–75

1 See S. Kramrisch in *Exploring India's Sacred Art*, Barbara Stoller Miller (ed.), pp. 114–15.
2 Sotheby's describe the dhurrie as made in Poona in 1924 for the Governor of Poona, but the sample in Ahmedabad has always remained in the jail and this dhurrie could only have been commissioned in Ahmedabad. Two similar dhurries were sold at Sotheby's: lot 23, inscribed Ann and Shirley twice, on 31 January 1974; and lot 68 on 10 October 1979.
3 See also Noah's *sura* in the holy Qur'an, *sura* LXXI Nuh or Noah.
4 See Zebrowski, *Deccani Paintings*, p. 9.
5 See Cohen, 'A Fearful Symmetry', in *Silk and Stone: The Third Hali Annual*, 1996, pp. 104–35.
6 The label in Persian and Hindi indicates that it was purchased in 1632 at the time of Mirza Raja Jai Singh I (1622–68) and was found in 1937 in one of the rooms in Amber Palace; see Vaish, *The Persian Garden Carpet in The Jaipur Museum*, p. 1. This example is also presumed to have been made in Kerman.
7 See Sotheby's sale of pictorial dhurries, a variation of Ark dhurries with aeroplane. Sale of Islamic Art and Carpets, 19 October 1983, lot 454.
8 See Zebrowski, *Deccani Paintings*, p. 218.
9 Ibid, p. 40.
10 See P. Jayakar, *Marg*, XV, 1962, p. 4.
11 See Vainker 'Silk of the Northern Song', pp. 173–75.
12 See Welch, *Flower From Every Meadow*, pp. 34–35.
13 Cohen refers to the figures as Europeans and mounted soldiers, see *The Unappreciated Dhurrie*, p. 26.
14 Cohen, *The Unappreciated Dhurrie*, p. 26.
15 Huyler, *Painted Prayers*, p. 53.
16 Ibid, p. 72.
17 See Twigg, *A Monograph on the Art & Practice of Carpet Making*, concerning superintendents moving from one jail to another and taking patterns with them.
18 Huyler, *Painted Prayers*, p. 14.
19 T. S. Maxwell, 'The Natural World', *In the Image of Man*, exhibition catalogue, Hayward Gallery, London, March–June 1982, p. 96.

20 Stupa I, Sanchi dating from the first century BC.
21 See Shankar and Housego, *Bridal Dhurries of India*, p. 135.
22 See Cohen, *The Unappreciated Dhurrie*, p. 14.

Chapter 3 Floral Dhurries pp. 76–85

1 See Walker, *Flowers Underfoot*, p. 95.
2 See Christies sale of Islamic art, Indian miniatures, rugs and carpets, 8 Oct 1991, lot 411.
3 See Ford, *Oriental Carpet Design*, p. 86.
4 Keene, lecture in May 2001, British Museum, *Some Regional Styles of Enamelling in the Mughal Period*.

Chapter 4 Medallion Dhurries pp. 86–109

1 See Guy and Swallow (eds), *Arts of India 1550–1900*, pp. 128–29.
2 See Cohen, 'Textiles' in *Islamic Heritage of the Deccan*, G. Michell (ed.), p. 120.
3 See Zebrowski, *Deccani Paintings*, p. 155.
4 See Cohen, 'Textiles', in *Islamic Heritage from the Deccan*, G. Michell (ed.), p. 120.
5 See sample from Jaipur jail, Ahuja, *Dhurrie*, p. 148.
6 See Cohen, *The Unappreciated Dhurrie*, p. 24.
7 Ibid.
8 Ibid.
9 See Ford, *Oriental Carpet Design*, p. 266.
10 See Cohen, *The Unappreciated Dhurrie*, pp. 20–21.
11 This was clearly demonstrated by Manuel Keene at a lecture on the subject in May 2001 at the British Museum, London.
12 The term East Turkestan applies to carpets produced in Yarkand, Kashgar and Khotan in the 18th to the early 20th century, in particular the cream, buff and indigo carpets.
13 Migrating tribes who finally settle in one province are often related such as the Qashaqai's, who are Turkic-speaking and relate to other Turkic-speaking tribes from north-western province, for instance the Qashqai's of Fars are probably related to the Shahsavan in northwest Iran. See Housego in *Tribal Rugs*, plate 69.
14 See Cohen, *The Unappreciated Dhurrie*, p. 58.

Chapter 5 Geometric Dhurries pp. 110–135

1 Cohen dates this particular dhurrie to the early 20th century in *The Unappreciated Dhurrie*, p. 30.
2 For a similar example see ibid, p. 40.
3 See Paris exhibition of 1925.
4 See Prasad, *Monograph on Carpet Making*.
5 See Blum, *The Fine Art of Textiles*, p. 129.
6 See Askari and Crill, *Colours of the Indus*, p. 51.
7 Geometric designs were particular to west Punjab because of the Muslim influence, while east Punjab had a more figurative tradition. See Gillow and Barnard, pp. 113–14.

Chapter 6 Prayer Dhurries pp. 136–153

1 See Sahai, *The Farrash Khana Hazoori Collection of Carpets...*, p. 1.
2 Lipton (ed.), *The Tiger Rugs of Tibet*, p. 15.
3 See Sahai, *The Farrash Khana Hazoori Collection of Carpets...*, p. 3.
4 See Pupul Jayakar in *Marg* XV, 1962, p. 4.
5 Ibid.
6 See Watt, *Indian Art at Delhi 1903*, pp. 432–33.
7 Ibid, pp. 445–46.
8 For a similar example see Ahuja, *Dhurrie*, p. 107.

9 See Schimmel in *Islamic Heritage of the Deccan*, G. Michell (ed.), p. 6.

10 I am indebted to Manijeh Bayani-Wolpert for deciphering and translating the inscription.

11 Ibid.

12 See Franses and Pinner, 'Dhurries, the Traditional Tapestries of India', *Hali*, 4, No. 3, pp. 241–42.

13 'Khwadja Mu'in al Din Hasan was the founder of the Chishtiyya order in India where he died in 1236. Shaykh Farid Gandj-Shakar and Ahaykh Nizam al Din Awliya' were essential in spreading the influence of the order to the whole of India. See *Encyclopaedia of Islam*, Brill et al., vol. II, pp. 49–56.

14 Dhikr-i Jahr, ibid.

15 'In the visual arts each note has a specific colour and other iconographic features' – see D. C. Bhattacharyya, 'Indian Subcontinent: Iconography' in Grove's *The Dictionary of Art*, vol. 15, p. 228.

16 See Brill, *Encyclopaedia of Islam*, 'Musalla', p. 659.

17 The adjective *samáwi* means both azure blue and the divine.

18 See Schimmel, 'The Celestial Garden', in Ettinghausen (ed.), *The Islamic Garden*, p. 15.

19 In this particular appellation I exclude Agra and Fatehpur Sikri which have none of the attributes of the rest of Uttar Pradesh.

20 Brill, *Encyclopaedia of Islam*, vol. II. p. 50.

21 For a similar example see Ahuja, *Dhurrie*, p. 110.

Glossary

abrash change of tone in a colour from using two separately dyed batches of yarn in weaving

asan mat or floor spread

bagh garden

bandhani tie-dye technique

bidri ware brass and silver inlaid into a dark zinc surface

bsat floor spread

chahar bagh or *char bagh* square plan garden divided into four quarters by canals

charkha wooden spinning wheel

charpai Indian bed made of wood and rope

chatai woven reed mat

chaupar medieval Indian game played with dice, precursor of Ludo

Chisti Sufi sect

darbar or *durbar* audience

dari, durrie or *dhurrie* a flatwoven cotton rug

Devi Hindu goddess

divan-i-khas audience hall

dovetailing or single-interlock weave technique used when a new colour is introduced within the same horizontal weft line. The warp which determines the separation of two different colour areas is used as a 'pole' from which the different coloured wefts are returned, leaving no gaps in the process. The weft of one colour area is turned back around the same warp as the weft from another colour area.

eccentric wefting or extra weft inserts weaving technique used for decorative purposes. It involves deliberately curving the wefts by beating down the weft unevenly and adding extra wefts to exaggerate the shape.

farrashkhana storehouse

flatweave technique in which individual wefts are woven over and under the warps

Ganesha Hindu elephant-headed god, remover of obstacles

Garuda mythical bird, vehicle of Vishnu

gopi milkmaid

guard stripe narrow band on each side of the main border of a rug

hamsa goose, vehicle of the god Brahma

haveli large mansion

heddle thread crossing warp to form loops and consolidating odd threads fastened to a shaft.

ikat resist-dyeing technique in which the threads of the warp or weft are dyed before weaving to create a pattern

jainamaz Muslim prayer dhurrie, single niche

jajim floor cover

jali pierced screen

Jami Masjid Congregational Mosque

kantha a quilted and embroidered cotton cover from Bengal

kesi Chinese silk panel of the northern Song dynasty

karkhana workshop

kathipa embroidery of floss silk on cotton

khes cotton woven shawl

kilim a flatwoven woollen rug

kolam Tamil word for floor decoration

Krishna Hindu Supreme Lord and Lover of Radha, an incarnation of Vishnu

Kufic early Arabic calligraphy

Lakshmi Hindu goddess of plenty and fertility

Mahabharata epic poem narrating the war in the kingdom of the Kurus

mandala geometric design with cosmic symbolism based on a circle inside a square

mahi fish (can be used as a weaving motif)

mandana floor decoration in Rajasthan

mihrab niche

mordant fixing agent used in dyeing

Mughals Muslim dynasty that ruled most of Northern India from the early 16th century until the mid-18th century

Nandi or *Nandin* Bull, mount of Shiva

palampore painted bed cover

panja weaving comb with metal teeth

pata scroll painting

patti additional top and bottom stripes in a dhurrie

pechwai painted cloth hanging

phulkari flowerwork embroidery

puja worship

Purna Kalasa Vase of Plenty

Radha consort of Krishna

raga word referring to mood and a particular dye in India

Ragamala series of paintings based on musical modes

Ramayana epic story of Rama and Lakshmana

rumal handkerchief or turban

saf Muslim prayer dhurrie, multi niche

satranji, satrangis or *suttringees* Hindustani word, sometimes used for flatweaves, meaning seven colours from *sat* (Hindi) meaning seven and *rang* (Persian) colour

selvedge binding of the rug closed by the weft loops and often in a different colour

semé scattering

shakti or *sakti* energetic aspect of a god occasionally personified as his wife

shed space between sets of warp threads

Shiva Hindu god who manifests himself in creative and destructive forms (cosmic energy)

sitalpatti cool mat from Bengal

slitweave a slit is formed vertically when the weft of one colour area is turned back around a warp parallel to another warp from which the weft from another colour area is turned, forming a gap. To prevent long vertical slits that can weaken the structure of the dhurrie, a crenellating or step effect is used to minimize the slits, and this to a certain extent dictates the design.

stupa Buddhist burial mound in a dome-like shape

Sufism Islamic mysticism

tabby weave or weft-faced plainweave the effect is produced when the number of weft threads is greater than the number of warps, hiding the generally undyed warps and therefore determining the colour of the weave.

talim numbered card used in weaving

Vedas ancient religious texts

Vishnu Hindu god of creation and preservation

Waqf Islamic Endowment Board

weft floats or weft-faced patterning as the name suggests, this involves the weaving of coloured wefts that appear only on the front face of the weave as part of a decorative pattern. The coloured weft floats at the back of the textile when not needed or used. This technique, a form of interlacing by skipping two or more warps, is often found in flatwoven saddlebags and other artefacts across Asia.

zilu flatweave produced on a draw loom

Select Bibliography

Abu'l-Fazl 'Allami', *A'in-i Akbari*, trans. H. Blochmann, New Delhi, 1977 (3rd edn)

——, *A'in-i Akbari*, Persian text, Delhi, 1855

Ahuja, S., M. Ahuja and M. Maluste, *Dhurrie: Flatwoven Rugs of India*, Mumbai, 1999

Archer, M., *Company Paintings, Indian Paintings of the British Period*, London, 1992

Archer, M., C. Rowell and R. Skelton, *Treasures from India: The Clive Collection at Powis Castle*, London, 1987

Askari, N., and L. Arthur, *Uncut Cloth*, London, 1999

Askari, N., and R. Crill, *Colours of the Indus: Costume and Textiles of Pakistan*, London, 1997

Baden-Powell, B. H., *Handbook of the Manufacturers and Arts of the Punjab*: vol. II, *Handbook of the Economic Products of the Punjab*, Lahore, 1872

Beach, M. C., and E. Koch (eds), *King of the World: The Padshahnama, An Imperial Mughal Manuscript from the Royal Library, Windsor Castle*, London, 1997

Begley, W. E., *Monumental Islamic Calligraphy from India*, Illinois, 1985

Behl, B. K., *The Ajanta Caves*, London, 1998

Bennett, I. (ed.), *Rugs and Carpets of the World*, London, 1977

Birdwood, G. C. M., *The Industrial Arts of India*, London, 1880; reprinted as *The Arts of India*, Delhi, 1988

Blum, D. E., *The Fine Art of Textiles: The Collections of the Philadelphia Museum of Art*, Philadelphia, 1997

Brill, E. J., et al., *Encylopaedia of Islam*, 1986 (first published 1905)

Burnell, Arthur Coke (ed.), *The Voyage of John Huyghen van Linshoten to the East Indies: From the old English translation of 1598*, New York, 1885

Chaghattai, A. M., *The Wazir Khan Mosque Lahore*, Lahore, 1975

Chanpawat. H. F. S., *Brief History of Jeypore*, Agra, 1899

Chattopadhyay, K., *Carpets and Floor Coverings of India*, Bombay, 1969

Cohen, S., 'A Fearful Symmetry: The Mughal Red-Ground "Grotesque" Carpets' in *Silk and Stone: The Art of Asia, The Third Hali Annual*, ed. J. Tilden, London, 1996

——, *The Development of Indian Floor-Coverings and their Appearance in Miniature Paintings*, PhD thesis, School of Oriental and African Studies, London, 1986

——, *The Unappreciated Dhurrie*, London, 1982

Cooper, I. *The Guide to Painted Towns of Shekhawati, Rajasthan* (no date)

Cooper, I., and J. Gillow, *Arts and Crafts of India*, London, 1996

Crill, R., *Indian Ikat Textiles*, London, 1998

Danielou, A., *Hindu Polytheism*, London, 1964

Davies, P., *The Tribal Eye, Antique Kilims of Anatolia*, New York, 1993

Della Valle, P., *The Travels of Pietro Della Valle in India from 1664*, trans. G. Havers, vol. II, London, 1892

Dhamija, J., *Indian Folk Arts and Crafts*, New Delhi, 1970

Dhamija. J. (ed.), *Crafts of Gujarat*, New York, 1985

Ellis, C. G., *Oriental Carpets in the Philadelphia Museum of Art*, Philadelphia, 1988

Emery, I., *The Primary Structures of Fabrics*, Washington, DC, 1966

Erdmann, K., *Oriental Rugs and Carpets: A Survey of Seven Centuries*, London, 1970

The Eye of the Courtier, Spink catalogue, London, 1999

Fawcett, C. G. H., *A Monograph on Dyes and Dyeing in the Bombay Presidency*, Bombay, 1896

Fisher, N. (ed.), *Mud, Mirror and Thread: Folk Traditions of Rural India*, Middletown, 1993

Ford, P. R. J., *Oriental Carpet Design: A Guide to Traditional Motifs, Patterns and Symbols*, London, 1981

Franses, M., and R. Pinner, 'Dhurries, the Traditional Tapestries of India', *Hali*, 4, No. 3, 1982

Gans-Ruedin, E., *Indian Carpets*, New York, 1984

Geijer, A., *A History of Textile Art*, London, 1979

Ghosh, P., E. Dimock and M. W. Meister, *Cooking for the Gods, The Art of Home Ritual in Bengal*, Philadelphia, 1995

Gillow, J., and N. Barnard, *Traditional Indian Textiles*, London, 1991

Gittinger, M., *Master Dyers to the World*, Washington, DC, 1982

Goswamy, B. N., *Essence of Indian Art*, San Francisco, 1986

Goswamy, B. N., and E. Fischer, *Wonders of a Golden Age, Painting at the Court of the Great Mughals*, Zurich, 1987

Gray, B., (ed.), *The Arts of India*, Oxford, 1981

Guy, J., and D. Swallow (eds), *Arts of India: 1550–1900*, London, 1990

Hacker, K. F., and K. J. Turnbull, *Courtyard, Bazaar, Temple: Traditions of Textile Expression in India*, Washington, DC, 1982

Haque, E., *Islamic Art Heritage of Bangladesh*, Dhaka, 1983

Harris, H. T., *Monograph on the Carpet Weaving Industry in South India*, Madras, 1908

Hendley, T. H., *Asian Carpets: 16th and 17th-Century Designs from the Jaipur Palaces*, London, 1905

Housego, *Tribal Rugs: An Introduction to the Weaving of the Tribes of Iran*, London, 1978

Huyler, S. P., *Gifts of Earth*, Middletown, 1996

——, *Painted Prayers, Women's Art in Village India*, London, 1994

——, *Village India*, New York, 1985

Imperial Gazetteer of India, *Rajputana*, Provincial Series, Calcutta, 1908

The Indian Heritage: Court Life and Arts under Mughal Rule, exhibition catalogue, Victoria and Albert Museum, London, 1982

In the Image of Man: The Indian Perception of the Universe through 2000 Years of Painting and Sculpture, exhibition catalogue, Hayward Gallery, London, 1982

Indian Folk Paintings, 15th to 19th century, from the Collection of Jagdish & Kamla Mittal Museum of Indian Art, exhibition catalogue, Hyderabad, New Delhi, 1990

Irwin, J., and M. Hall, *Indian Embroideries: Historic Textiles of India at the Calico Museum*, vol. II, Ahmedabad, 1973

——, *Indian Painted and Printed Fabrics: Historic Textiles of India at the Calico Museum*, vol. I, Ahmedabad, 1971

Jain, K. A., and J. Jain (eds), *The Jaipur Album or All About Jaipur*, Jaipur, 1935

Jaitly, J., *The Craft Traditions of India*, New Delhi, 1990

Keene, M., *Some Regional Styles of Enamelling in the Mughal Period: Their Inheritance and Bequests*, unpublished lecture, British Museum, London, May 2001

Koch, E., *Mughal Architecture*, Munich, 1991

Kramrisch, S., *The Presence of S'iva*, Princeton, 1981

Kramrisch, S., and B. Stoler Miller, *Exploring India's Sacred Art*, Philadelphia, 1983

Krishna, N., *Arts and Crafts of Tamilnadu*, Ahmedabad and Middletown, 1992

Latimer, C., *Monograph on Carpet Making in the Punjab, 1905–06*, Lahore, 1907

Lipton, M. (ed.), *The Tiger Rugs of Tibet*, London, 1988

Michell, G. (ed.), *Islamic Heritage of the Deccan*, Bombay, 1986

Mohanty, B. C., K. V. Chandramouli and H. D. Naik, *Natural Dyeing Processes of India*, Ahmedabad, 1987

Mohanty, B.C., and J. P. Mohanty, *Block-Printing and Dyeing of Bagaru, Rajasthan*, Ahmedabad, 1983

Mukerji, N. G., *A Monograph on Carpet Weaving in Bengal*, Calcutta, 1907

Mukharji, T. N., *Art Manufactures of India*, Calcutta, 1888

Phillips, B., *Tapestry*, London, 1994

Platts, J. T., *A Dictionary of Urdu, Classical Hindi and English*, Oxford, 1884 (reprinted Delhi, 1997)

Prasad, K., *Monograph on Carpet Making in the United Provinces*, Allahabad, 1907

Rakesh, P., and K. Lewis, *Shekhawati, Rajasthan's Painted Homes*, Delhi, 1995

Report on the Administration of the Bikaner State 1893–94, prepared by Rai Bahadur Sodhi Hukm Singh, Vice-President of the Regency Council of Bikaner, Bikaner, The Central Jail Press.

Report on the Administration of the Jaipur State for 1922–23, 1923– 24, and 1925-26, Part I, (confidential), Allahabad 1927 (Dr Y. Sahai Library)

Roe, Sir Thomas, *The Embassy of Sir Thomas Roe to India, 1615–1619*, ed. Sir William Foster, London, 1926

Safrani, S. H. (ed.), *Golconda and Hyderabad*, Bombay, 1992

Sahai, Y., *Maharaja Sawai Ram Singh II of Jaipur: The Photographer Prince*, Jaipur 1996

——, 'Carpet Weaving at Jaipur Jail: The Early Years' in *Carpet News: Journal of Carpet Industry*, vol. 4, no. 5, Sept.–Oct., Jaipur, 1980

——, *The Farrash Khana Hazoori Collection of Carpets of Mirza Raja Jai Singh I of Amber (Jaipur)*, with notes on *Early Flooring used in India*, Jaipur

Sarana, G., Munshi, *Census Report for Jaipur State*, Lucknow, 1903 (Dr Y. Sahai Library)

Schimmel, A., 'The Celestial Garden' in *The Islamic Garden*, ed. Ettinghausen, Washington, DC, 1976

Sen, P., *Crafts of West Bengal*, Ahmedabad, 1994

Serjeant, R. B., 'Material for a History of Islamic Textiles up to the Mongol Conquest', in *Ars Islamica*, vols IX–XV, Michigan, 1942–51

Shankar, A., and J. Housego, *Bridal Durries of India*, Ahmedabad, 1997

Soustiel, J., *La Céramique Islamique*, Paris, 1985

Stein, A., *Ancient Khotan: Detailed report of archaeological explorations in Chinese Turkestan*, 2 vols., Oxford, 1907

Stowers, H. L., Lt. Col., *Notes on Jaipur*, Jaipur, 1909; 2nd edn, Oct 1916 (Dr Y. Sahai Library)

Tavernier, J-B., *Travels in India*, trans. V. Ball, London, 1889; 2nd edn, London, 1975

Tillotson, G. H. R., *The Rajput Palaces: The Development of an Architectural Style, 1450–1750*, London and New Haven, 1987

Twigg, H., *A Monograph on the Art and Practice of Carpet Making in the Bombay Presidency*, Bombay, 1907

Vainker, S., 'Silk of the Northern Song', in *Silk & Stone: The Art of Asia, The Third Hali Annual*, London, 1996

Vaish, H. P., *The Persian Garden Carpet in The Jaipur Museum*, Jaipur, 1946

Verma, T., *Karkhanas under the Mughals, from Akbar to Aurangzeb: A Study in Economic Development*, Delhi, 1994

Walker, D., *Flowers Underfoot, Indian Carpets of the Mughal Era*, New York, 1997; London, 1998

——, 'Classical Indian Rugs', *Hali*, 4, No. 3, 1982

Watson, J. Forbes, *The Textile Fabrics of India*, London, 1866

Watt, G., *Indian Art at Delhi 1903, being the Official Catalogue of the Delhi Exhibition, 1902–1903*, Calcutta 1903

Welch, S. C., *India: Art and Culture 1300–1900*, New York, 1985

——, *Imperial Mughal Painting*, London, 1978

——, *A Flower from Every Meadow*, New York, 1973

Yacopino, F., *Threadlines Pakistan*, Islamabad, 1977

Yule, H., and A. C. Burnell, *Hobson-Jobson: A Glossary of Anglo-Indian Colloquial Words and Phrases*, London, 1886 (reprinted Delhi, 2000)

Zebrowski, M., *Deccani Painting*, London, 1983

Ziauddin, M., *A Monograph on Moslem Calligraphy*, Lahore

Zimmer, H., *Myths and Symbols in Indian Art and Civilization*, New York, 1946

Acknowledgments

For the last ten years I have been pursuing the study of dhurries, I have met numerous people who have contributed greatly to my research and made this book possible. It would take another chapter to name them all, but they know who they are and I thank them all. However, I would like particularly to acknowledge my debt to Mitchell Crites, Ralph Pinder-Wilson and Nahla Nassar whose encouragement, help and critical observations have been instrumental, and Jamie Govier for giving his time and producing great photography.

This study could not have been realized without the permission of the authorities in both India and Pakistan to visit the jails and photograph the relevant archives. I would like to thank the home ministers, the head of jails and the superintendents of the numerous prisons I visited for their assistance and their trust in allowing me into high-security areas for the purpose of my research.

I also would like to thank the curators and staff of museums in both India and Pakistan who have been extremely helpful and generous with their time and who have allowed me to reproduce objects from their collections.

I am also very grateful to the kindness, warmth and hospitality of my many friends in India and Pakistan who have made my stays over the years memorable.

I wish to thank private individuals, collectors, institutions and museums who have allowed me to reproduce objects form their collections and who have been sympathetic to my requests.

My many thanks to the staff at Thames and Hudson who have made this book possible.

Finally my greatest debt to my mother whose curiosity initiated this whole pursuit, and to John-William and Marie-Louise who helped with the filing of my numerous photographs and put up with my long absences, and to Aart my gratitude.

Photo Credits

Photographs by Nada Chaldecott

Picture numbers: *4, 6, 11, 19, 22, 23, 24, 25, 27, 28, 29, 31, 32, 33, 34, 35, 36, 38, 39, 43, 44, 45, 46, 47, 48, 49, 51, 69, 76, 80, 103, 105, 106, 108, 112, 119, 124, 132, 133, 134, 135, 137, 146, 148, 149, 151, 155, 157, 158, 162, 172, 173, 176, 183, 184, 185, 186, 192, 195, 196, 204, 211, 228, 233, 240, 241, 250.*

Photographs by Jamie Govier

Picture numbers: *2, 3, 20, 40, 41, 42, 50, 52, 55, 57, 58, 59, 60, 63, 64, 65, 66, 67, 68, 71, 72, 73, 74, 75, 79, 85, 87, 88, 92, 96, 97, 98, 101, 107, 111, 115, 118, 120, 123, 127, 130, 131, 140, 141, 142, 143, 145, 150, 153, 159, 160, 161, 163, 168, 169, 177, 179, 180, 181, 182, 187, 189, 190, 191, 197, 198, 199, 200, 201, 202, 205, 206, 207, 208, 209, 213, 214, 215, 217, 218, 219, 220, 222, 223, 224, 225, 226, 229, 230, 231, 232, 235, 236, 237, 238, 239, 242, 243, 245, 246, 247, 248, 249.*

All © 2003 Nada Chaldecott

Index

Page numbers in *italic* indicate illustration captions.

tabby weave

slitweave

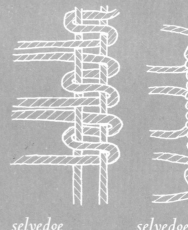

selvedge
tied ground weft

selvedge
parallel wrapping

weft-faced plainweave

curved wefts

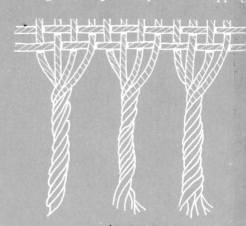

warp loop fringe

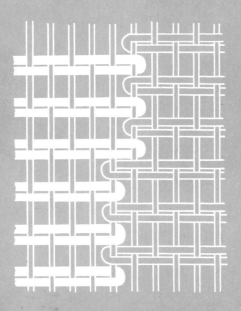

dovetailing

countered weft twining

net fringe

interlocking

wrapping with coloured weft

plaited fringe